FUNDAMENTALS OF SCHOOL SCHEDULING

Fundamentals of School Scheduling

Gwen Schroth

with contributions from
Anita Pankake and **Paul Terry**

LANCASTER · BASEL

Fundamentals of School Scheduling
a TECHNOMIC publication

Published in the Western Hemisphere by
Technomic Publishing Company, Inc.
851 New Holland Avenue, Box 3535
Lancaster, Pennsylvania 17604 U.S.A.

Distributed in the Rest of the World by
Technomic Publishing AG
Missionsstrasse 44
CH-4055 Basel, Switzerland

Copyright © 1997 by Technomic Publishing Company, Inc.
All rights reserved

No part of this publication may be reproduced, stored in a
retrieval system, or transmitted, in any form or by any means,
electronic, mechanical, photocopying, recording, or otherwise,
without the prior written permission of the publisher.

Printed in the United States of America
10 9 8 7 6 5 4 3 2 1

Main entry under title:
 Fundamentals of School Scheduling

A Technomic Publishing Company book
Bibliography: p. 119
Includes index p. 127

Library of Congress Catalog Card No. 97-61109
ISBN No. 1-56676-575-7

To my husband, Richard, who listened, counseled, and guided me throughout the production of this book.

CONTENTS

Prologue ix

Introduction xi

1. INSTRUCTION 1
Instruction: A Priority 1
Responding to Student Needs 3
Appropriate Curriculum and Instruction 6
Staff Development: A Change Issue 10
Staff Development and Scheduling Choices 14
References 16

2. CHANGE 19
Introduction 19
What Can Be Done to Prepare for Change? 21
What to Expect When Change Occurs 26
What Actions Can Help in Preparing for Change and
   in Successfully Managing the Change Process? 33
References 37

3. MEETING CHALLENGES, FACING PROBLEMS 39
Considerations for All Scheduling Models 40
Additional Considerations 46
Advantages and Disadvantages of Various
   Scheduling Models 50
References 62

4. CONSTRUCTING THE SCHEDULE 65
Constructing a Master Schedule: Traditional Models 65

Block Scheduling Models 82
The Teaming Model 87
References 90

5. FLEXIBLE SCHEDULING FOR ELEMENTARY SCHOOLS 91

A Rationale for Change at the Elementary Level 91
The Case for Longer Class Periods 93
Flexible Scheduling at the Elementary Level 96
Guidelines for Block Scheduling 101
References 104

Appendix A: Computer Programs 107

Appendix B: Frequently Asked Questions 115

Bibliography 119

Index 127

PROLOGUE

In the summer of 1989, during an interview for a middle school principalship, the superintendent asked if I knew how to construct a schedule. I indicated I could, considering scheduling is a fairly simple task. After all, I had jumped the usual hurdles that elementary principals experience. The school also had two able counselors who had worked with scheduling in the past.

I could not have been more naive. For a month before school opened, the counselors and I worked seven days a week, late into the night, struggling to refine the master schedule so that the 800 students could be placed into classes. Despite our efforts, for the first two weeks of school, twenty to thirty students sat in the auditorium each period, waiting for schedules. Teachers complained that some classes had forty students while others had only ten or twelve. The job got done, but many students were in courses where they had no business being, and some teachers had more students than chairs during some periods of the day.

Ready for change, I attended a scheduling workshop conducted by Bob Hanson, currently with McGraw Hill School Systems, talked to other principals, and met with teachers to gain enough knowledge to sensibly and efficiently bring together students and teachers each period of every day. The counselors, assistant principal, secretaries, teachers, and even some parents became experts at finding strategies to refine the scheduling process. This book is a result of those efforts by the staff at Greenville Texas Middle School. The hope is that others will profit from what we learned.

GWEN SCHROTH

INTRODUCTION

Time is the most valuable thing a man can spend.
—Diogenes Laertius

The Bird of Time has but a little way to fly—and Lo!
the Bird is on the wing.
—Edward Fitzgerald (1879)

The goal of current restructuring and reform in education is ultimately to improve student achievement. Yet, decisions about change do not always emanate from within schools. Judgments about how much time and how that time is to be spent, for example, often originate with courts, legislatures, state departments, and local boards. Many of these decisions have significantly influenced schools and classroom schedules.

On the federal level, the Individuals with Disabilities Education Act of 1990 and the more recent interpretation of Section 504 of the 1973 Rehabilitation Act have resulted in the expectation that every teacher can and should make time to address the needs of every student, regardless of the student's physical or mental ability. A legislative example is Texas's House Bill 72, adopted in 1984, as a reform measure, which went so far as to mandate the exact number of minutes each subject was to be taught each day. Also at the state level, some departments of education have insisted that schools adopt site-based management, which requires staff and administrator time for successful implementation. And, local school boards may determine how many students a teacher will teach, how long the school day will be, and how many minutes children will spend at recess.

These decisions, made from outside school walls, often fail to include directions for utilization of instructional time. Yet, time is a finite resource. Teachers are asking how they are to meet the increasing demands upon their time while maintaining the goal of increasing student achievement. A report from the National Education Association's Special Committee on Time Resources (as cited in Dalheim, 1994) states that "Across the nation in schools and districts engaged in transforming schools into more effective learning communities, the issue that has emerged as the most intense and the one that universally dominates discussion is time. . . . In a recent *Education Week* series, time was identified as one of seven key areas where change must occur for school reform to succeed" (p. 9). Dalheim then quotes Sommerfeld, from the same series, as saying, "We Have Met the Enemy, and They Are Hours."

Thus, in an effort to spend the "time budget" more wisely, elementary and middle schools are turning to more flexible arrangements. "Block scheduling," "team teaching," and "interdisciplinary instruction" have become common terms and reflect an effort to reorganize and restructure the use of time. Orchestrating the school day to make the best use of time in achieving instructional goals places increased demands on administrators as they schedule the school day.

The ability of the school administrator to schedule teachers' and students' time so that each receives the most from each school day has become an essential skill. It is here that conceptualizing, organizing, and carrying out detailed planning is most visible. If well done, the schedule will strongly support the instructional and curricular program of the school. On the other hand, if poorly designed, the schedule will be a roadblock to a balanced curriculum and instructional flexibility (Ubben & Hughes, 1992).

WHY THIS BOOK

The National Council for the Accreditation of Teacher Education (NCATE) provides guidelines for educational leadership training for principals. Within the guidelines, Area III, Organizational Leadership, has direct implications for scheduling. This area calls for principals to acquire the knowledge, skills, and attributes to understand and improve the organization and to implement operational plans (Houston et al.,

1995). Consequently, this book has been prepared for school administrators at the elementary and middle school levels who need appropriate management techniques for scheduling students into classes. All of the parts of the puzzle will be presented so that the administrator, in piecing them together, can make wise choices regarding the configuration of the school day and implement those decisions efficiently.

The material here is primarily for three groups: (a) The beginning principal, (b) those principals wishing to move either from the elementary to the secondary or from the secondary to the elementary level, and (c) administrators planning to change their scheduling formats, for example, moving to block scheduled, interdisciplinary teams. Pogrow (1996) suggests that practitioners passionately want to help young people and can use assistance in implementing reform. Designing, planning, and implementing any form of scheduling, even the traditional 50-minute period class, is complex. This book can serve as a guide.

The aspiring principal has an added incentive to carefully consider the full gamut of issues surrounding scheduling. Frequently, when interviewed for an administrative position, prospective principals are on the spot to address scheduling-related concerns. This book's presentation should prepare interviewees to speak with authority about creating the master schedule and accompanying issues such as instructional time, implementing change, staff development, and faculty involvement.

Although discussing a variety of scheduling formats, no one particular type is advocated, because many factors influence such a choice. Budget, student needs, teacher preferences, as well as parent and community desires impact this decision. As a result, scheduling becomes a reflection of each school's unique needs. Year-long scheduling is not addressed.

The first chapter directs attention to the instructionally related issue of students' needs, effective teaching practices, staff development, and special populations, focusing on how these relate to scheduling. Chapter 2 details the impact of change on schools and outlines steps for successfully bringing about reform. Chapter 3 discusses the many scheduling-related issues with which a principal must be concerned and presents the advantages and disadvantages of various scheduling options. Chapter 4 describes the process involved in creating a master schedule. Finally, Chapter 5 strives to meet the scheduling-related needs of the elementary principal.

HISTORICAL PERSPECTIVE

Although the current burst of interest in redesigning the school day appears innovative, the concept of maximizing use of time through reorganization is not new. Several decades ago, experiments challenged traditional scheduling of elementary students into contained classrooms and secondary students rotating from class to class for 45- to 50-minute class periods. Some of these new configurations failed, but remnants linger in the more flexible arrangements of time and staff. A brief summary of the historical background of scheduling provides a basis for better understanding what is occurring in schools today. Lessons learned from the past provide the building blocks for today's successes.

In the early 19th century, teachers typically had a limited education and were expected to function well in all subject areas. Much as elementary teachers today, staff at all levels might teach any subject at any time of the day. In the late 1800s, the Carnegie Unit of approximately 50-minute class periods, in which a single subject is taught and for which teachers specialize in particular subject areas, became the most frequently used scheduling format. This continues to be common in secondary schools. With the division of K–12 schools into elementary, junior high, and high schools, the Carnegie Unit was extended to the junior high schools, which were viewed as mini-high schools.

Similarly, elementary schools have blocked periods of time for particular subjects. Unlike middle level schools, elementary school students are placed with the self-contained classroom teacher for the full day. The full-day, one-teacher arrangement opened the door for an important change at the elementary level, the blurring of distinctions between subject areas. Interdisciplinary instruction is becoming more widely adopted at middle as well as elementary schools.

A major change in scheduling the staff's as well as the students' day was introduced in 1958, after J. Lloyd Trump first published "An Image of the Future" (Trump, 1958). Holleman (1974) and Trump (1977) describe the radical plan as having three major components: (a) large group (40–150 students) experiences for approximately 30 minutes for motivational purposes, (b) small group reaction and discussion periods for motivation and clarification, lasting also about 30 minutes, and (c) independent study, individually or in groups of three to ten at home, school, or in the community. Instruction was ungraded, and time and space were flexible to allow changes in grouping. The plan failed, partly due to the large amount of unstructured, independent study time for students that they were unable to use profitably.

The Trump Plan did bring to education a clear recognition that (a) some learning activities require more time than others, (b) lectures must be limited, (c) some subjects require daily meetings, and (d) class size can be a variable in the effectiveness of the instructional activity. The Trump Plan also introduced the differentiated staffing concept of groups of teachers, instructional assistants, clerks, aides, specialists, and community consultants working together as teams.

The notion that flexibility in scheduling and use of facilities is beneficial to staff and students led to another unusual experiment in the 1970s: the open school concept (Hurt, 1992). New elementary school buildings did not have divisions between classrooms. Students were able to progress at their own speed, moving from one grade area to another, depending on their progress. Teachers functioned as cooperative teams who facilitated such individualized instruction. The open school concept aroused considerable dissatisfaction for two reasons—the first, pressure from parents who did not support the concept; and second, failure of teachers to implement the concept as they had been trained. Schools soon began to build walls, and new schools had self-contained classrooms again.

In the 1960s and 1970s, with individualized instruction a continued priority, some schools began to modify the lock-step, seven-period day. Termed "modular flexible scheduling," the plan was to provide greater variability in scheduling time, space, teachers, and students (Wood, Nicholson, & Findley, 1985; Hughes & Ubben, 1980). Dividing the school day into 21 modules of 20 minutes in length, or 105 modules weekly, the plan suggested combining modules to vary class lengths and sizes as needed. The schedule could change from day to day.

Educators found two major problems with modular scheduling (Ubben, 1976). Once the 20-minute modules were divided into workable time periods, teachers tended to lock into those units, failing to make use of the opportunity for flexibility. As with the Trump Plan, discipline problems stemmed from students having long periods of unscheduled time when they were expected to engage in independent study. Ubben aptly questioned the likelihood of student accountability.

In 1964, Beggs described team teaching as combining the talents of staff in the effort to improve instruction, and Keefe (1971) applauded the interdisciplinary model, portraying it as a plan that makes maximum use of teacher potential, comparing it to the hopes that schools have for providing for individual differences of students. With today's widely adopted middle school concept, teaming has finally found its place and is flourishing.

In the 1970s, with flexibility continuing to be a high priority, fluid-block scheduling became popular in junior high schools (Hughes & Ubben, 1980; Ubben, 1976). This scheduling pattern, evident in middle schools today, allots a block of two to three hours to interdisciplinary teams of teachers to schedule instruction according to students' needs, hence the term *fluid*. A variety of options was recommended; for example, two social studies teachers, paired with two language arts teachers could control the use of a three-hour block of time with their assigned 120 students. Another option was allowing a team to schedule an interdisciplinary unit with each teacher contributing to a specialized part of an overall common topic. Any type of fluid-block scheduling could incorporate several single-hour courses during the course of the day.

In the 1970s, Wood, Nicholson, and Findley (1979) proposed other somewhat unusual and less popular alternatives to the conventional Carnegie Unit of fixed length. The revolving-period schedule moved one particular period to different times each week so no one class suffered from such interruptions as assemblies or pep rallies. Still another plan designed to provide flexibility, the period-flexible schedule, provided a daily change in the length of each period, alternating between 30, 60, and 90 minutes. Thus, teachers could plan for at least one activity each week that required a longer segment of time. Another model was the modular schedule, fashioned along Trump's plan, which broke the day into 14-minute segments allowing for a variety of choices, for example, 14-, 28-, or even 70-minute blocks of time for a class. Still another configuration was the daily demand schedule. A complex arrangement, the schedule changed daily depending on faculty needs, and it required planning with the full-time scheduling coordinator three days in advance.

Another scheduling alternative, popular in the late 1980s and early 1990s, which continues to be effective in middle and high schools today, is the Zero Period schedule. Offered as a solution for older students' scheduling problems, designated courses begin an hour earlier than the regular school day and allow students to leave an hour earlier or enroll in an extra class. This design alters teachers' schedules and allows students more flexibility.

The publication of *Turning Points* (Carnegie Council on Adolescent

Development, 1989) brought major changes for middle level schools. Recognizing that junior high schools were simply mirror images of high schools, the Carnegie Council recommended that schools be reconfigured to fit the developmental needs of young adolescents. The traditional schedule seemed to be a major obstacle to providing the desired gradual transition from elementary to high school. The Council found that moving from the stability of the primary classroom to a setting with six or even seven class changes a day left young people feeling lost. The Carnegie Report asserted that students need time to learn and to develop relationships with caring adults in order to achieve. With this recommendation, various forms of block scheduling and interdisciplinary teaming took hold in middle schools across the country. The earlier work by Trump and other researchers provided the preliminary work on which these schools could base their changes. With block scheduling, teachers are given longer periods of time, usually 90 minutes but as much as a half or a whole day, to work with students in one subject. Teaming is an arrangement where a group of teachers, usually four or five, works with 125 to 150 students, creating a school within a school. Teaming can be combined with block scheduling or operate with traditional 45- to 50-minute class periods. Either way, interdisciplinary units of study can be developed to aid students' understanding of connections between subjects.

Some recurring themes emerge from this history of experimentation. The first is the perceived need for flexibility for teachers as well as students. The second is the emphasis on individualized instruction. The third is the principle that teachers working cooperatively together benefits students. These themes are apparent today in the growing popularity of alternative-scheduling formats, in the oft-cited slogan, "All Children Can Learn," and in the rapid move toward teaming and shared decision making. Although not new, these themes are taking on new meaning as educators seek to ensure that change takes place on all levels, from staff development and instructional delivery to inclusion of the staff, parents, and community in scheduling decisions.

REFERENCES

Beggs, D. W. III. (1964). *A practical application of the Trump Plan.* Englewood Cliffs, NJ: Prentice-Hall.

Carnegie Council on Adolescent Development. (1989). *Turning points: Preparing Ameri-*

can youth for the 21st century. The report of the task force on education of young adolescents. New York: Carnegie Council on Adolescent Development.

Dalheim, M. (1994). *Time strategies.* West Haven, CT: National Education Association of the United States.

Holleman, I. T., Jr. (1974). *The Trump Plan and the utilization of the differentiated staff* (NIE Publication No. EA 008 559, pp. 2–19). Washington, DC: U.S. Department of Health, Education and Welfare.

Houston, P. D., Carter, G. R., Sava, S. G., & Dyer, T. J. (1995). *NCATE guidelines: Curriculum guidelines for advanced programs in educational leadership for principals, superintendents, curriculum directors, and supervisors.* Alexandria, VA: Association for Supervision and Curriculum Development.

Hughes, L. W., & Ubben, G. C. (1980). *The secondary principal's handbook.* Boston: Allyn & Bacon.

Hurt, J. (1992). Opening Pandora's box. *Educational Facility Planner, 30*(3), 14–18.

Keefe, J. W. (1971, January). *Differentiated staffing – Its rewards and pitfalls.* Paper presented at the National Association of Secondary School Principals Annual Convention, Houston, TX.

Pogrow, S. (1996, June). Reforming the wannabe reformers: Why education reforms almost always end up making things worse. *Phi Delta Kappan, 77*(10), 656–663.

Sommerfeld, M. (1993, March 13). Time and space. *Education Week*, 13–19.

Trump, J. L. (1958, April). An image of the future in improved staff utilization. *Bulletin of the National Association of Secondary School Principals, XLII*, 324–329.

Trump, J. L. (1977). *School for everyone.* Reston, VA: National Association for Secondary School Principals.

Ubben, G. C. (1976). A third block schedule. *NASSP Bulletin, 60*(397), 104–111.

Ubben, G. C., & Hughes, L. W. (1992). *The principal* (2nd ed.). Boston: Allyn & Bacon.

Wood, C. L., Nicholson, E. W., & Findley, D. G. (1979). *The secondary school principal: Manager and supervisor.* Boston: Allyn & Bacon.

Wood, C. L., Nicholson, E. W., & Findley, D. G. (1985). *The secondary school principal: Manager and supervisor.* Boston: Allyn & Bacon.

CHAPTER 1

Instruction

New occasions teach new duties.
—James Russell Lowell

I am not willing that this discussion should close without mention of the value of a true teacher.
—Henry Brooks Adams

INSTRUCTION: A PRIORITY

A book on scheduling would seemingly begin by describing the step-by-step process for building a master schedule, weaving in all of the details for consideration along the way. Such an ordering would be similar to building a house roof first, expecting to pour the foundation at a convenient later date. Preliminary to constructing a schedule is the foundation work of assessing student needs, examining what teachers are doing, and ensuring that classroom instruction is improving student achievement. After teachers have made instruction optimally effective for students, it is appropriate to consider how use of time could further enhance achievement.

Some educators have discovered that ordering of events is necessary. The staff of a middle school in Oregon, seeking to spend time more wisely, began by investigating a variety of scheduling models. To their surprise, they had to identify instructional goals before they could deal with organizational issues such as scheduling (Kentta, 1993). The school schedule, they found, must be designed to support, not drive, the instructional program. In another part of the country, a new principal found middle school teachers' instructional methods sorely in need of improvement (Schroth & Dunbar, 1993). Scheduling techniques, likewise, were outdated. While more efficient scheduling was an obvious necessity, how and what teachers taught was a clear priority. In this school, streamlining the scheduling process allowed more students to be placed in courses of their choice, teachers to have balanced numbers of students in their classes, and school to open smoothly in the fall, but what took place in the classroom most directly effected higher student achievement, teacher morale, and parent satisfaction.

Attending to instruction is supported by Pogrow (1996) when he states that the ultimate reality is that the only way to improve education significantly is by the use of more powerful forms of curricula in the hands of very good teachers who are trained to teach better. As teaching improves, how the configuration of the school day can support and become a driving force behind instruction, rather than the reverse, becomes more evident.

In some schools, principals focus on one effort, scheduling, without considering it in the light of instruction. Sarason (1990) warns that to focus on only one part of, or group in, the education system, independent of how that part conditions and is conditioned by others, immediately reduces the chances of achieving goals. In these schools, administrators seem to expect that changes in instruction will inevitably find their way into the classroom as new scheduling formats are implemented. True, some teachers may already use techniques necessary for nontraditional time configurations such as cooperative learning, conflict management, or interdisciplinary methods. Unfortunately, though, not all teachers perfect these methods; many continue to teach much as they always have. Scheduling reforms alone cannot produce real academic gains.

Other principals wisely take time to train their faculty in new teaching methods before considering major school reform. As teachers become more innovative and experimental in their classroom activities, they adopt flexible and cooperative approaches that demand new organizational arrangements, one of which may be altered configurations of the school day, including scheduling. In these schools, the transition to a new type of schedule is driven by the teachers and based on instructional considerations. Change, in this case, is likely to be smooth as teachers find the new schedule furthers their attempts to improve instructionally.

Merenbloom (1991) emphasizes that teachers preparing to work with middle school students should become very familiar with (1) the needs of the students, (2) an appropriate curriculum model, and (3) a variety of options for organizing schools for effective instruction. Such advice is equally important to administrators seeking to become instructional leaders. This chapter addresses the first two—the needs of students and appropriate curriculum and instruction—and shows their relationship to scheduling. Related staff-development issues are included as well. Suggestions for additional staff development for nontraditional scheduling formats are also listed. Number three, options for organizing schools for effective instruction, is discussed in Chapter 3.

RESPONDING TO STUDENT NEEDS

What and how teachers teach should be a response to what students need. For example, elementary and middle school students are restless; they have short attention spans and require physical movement every 15 to 20 minutes. Instruction should therefore include interaction with the material and frequent changes in activity. Such changes are facilitated by a schedule that allows teachers to change settings, rearrange subject matter, and regroup students. This section illustrates the important relationship between student needs and time allotment.

Elementary students are usually placed in classrooms where they interact with one teacher for an entire day. This practice provides the stability and nurturance that small children require. Middle school students generally move from class to class and teacher to teacher as do high schoolers, which requires these preadolescents to interact daily with six or more adults in a variety of settings. The largely publicized Carnegie Report, in *Turning Points* (Carnegie Council on Adolescent Development, 1989), claimed that middle level students are not young high schoolers, but they have unique natures requiring specialized educational approaches. Some of these approaches resemble those practiced in high schools, others are like elementary school strategies. Because each of these groups of students is unique, this chapter addresses each separately.

Elementary Student Needs

Most chidren are excited about their first years in school but are dependent on teachers to create an environment favorable to their development. Young children's environmental and cultural experiences help to determine the direction of their physical, emotional, and intellectual growth. The classroom setting and curriculum must engage the whole child. Chapter 5 provides detailed discussion of scheduling for elementary students.

PHYSICAL DEVELOPMENT

Elementary children grow at a slow, steady pace. Their attention spans are short, and their large muscle coordination is far better than their fine motor skills. Children develop concepts about the world through active physical interaction with their environment in contrast to the more passive learning of adults. They must therefore be physically involved in the learning. Schedules should allow teachers the flexibility and creativity of moving from one setting to another or changing plans without disrupting other classrooms.

SOCIAL/EMOTIONAL DEVELOPMENT

While having friends and peer groups is the most powerful socializing force for elementary students (Black, Puckett, & Bell, 1992), young children need a caring, consistent relationship with significant adults. Carl Rogers (as cited by Black, Puckett, & Bell, 1992) states that elementary students are in the developmental stages of determining a sense of self; adults establish close relationships with young children by building on their strengths and capabilities. Teachers are significant adults, and establishing relationships requires them to spend long periods of time with students. The school day should be structured to encourage bonding among students and among students and teachers. Scheduling long periods of uninterrupted time allows teachers to build relationships with students and students to learn socially acceptable ways of interacting with one another and to develop trust through monitored cooperative activities.

INTELLECTUAL DEVELOPMENT

Elementary schoolchildren are in an intense stage of intellectual development. They acquire the building blocks in the early grades: reading, use of language, numbers, and writing. As children's memories are not yet fully developed, learning basic skills can be confusing; integrating subject areas can promote transfer so that learning becomes more permanent. For example, teaching reading in conjunction with writing or including music or physical education in thematic, interdisciplinary units reinforces long-term memory. Interdisciplinary teaching requires time for teachers to coordinate their instructional activities; they must have a common planning period.

Needs of the Middle School Student

The early adolescent goes through a number of life changes—physically, mentally, socially, and emotionally—all in a brief period of time. Unlike younger children, preadolescents are fully conscious of the changes taking place within them. Middle school students are stereotypically seen as restless, in perpetual movement, and shifting in their seats (Lorain, 1996). Young adolescents experience phenomenal growth spurts so that it simply hurts to sit still very long.

PHYSICAL NEEDS

Early adolescents (a) have an increase in muscle size and strength, (b) develop at varying rates with girls about two years ahead of boys, (c) begin puberty earlier than prior generations, (d) are relatively free from illness, and (e) are ungainly and awkward due to growth spurts. Although their tendency toward lassitude was once considered a physical issue, it is now recognized as psychological (George & Lawrence, 1982).

Consequently, the school's schedule must include regular and frequent opportunities to appropriately channel energy. Changing classes, physical education classes, and lunch periods all provide for movement. Permitting quiet movement about the classroom, shortening periods of time when students are seated at desks, and changing groups within and between classrooms help. Activities that include problem solving, manipulating, constructing, reconstructing, and experimenting physically engage students as well.

SOCIAL/EMOTIONAL DEVELOPMENT

Charity James (as cited in George & Lawrence, 1982) highlights the strongly conflicting emotions of middle school students by stating their needs in pairs of opposites.

- a need to be needed
- a need to need

- a need to move inward
- a need for intensity
- a need for myth and legend
- a need for physical activity
- a need for separateness
- a need to affect the outer world
- a need for routine
- a need for fact
- a need for stillness
- a need for belonging

Scheduling time for interaction at lunch, before and after school, and during advisory periods addresses the social/emotional needs of students. Intramural sports, cooperative learning groups, and peer tutoring allow for individual goals to be attained through group efforts while also providing for development of positive interpersonal relationships. Interacting with local leaders and engaging in community service projects address the needs of middle schoolers. If carried out correctly, many of these activities take more than the typical 50-minute class period but are possible when a schedule includes at least an occasional class of 90 or more minutes.

MENTAL/INTELLECTUAL NEEDS

Young adolescents are often immature, caught up in their own immediate concrete experiences, and unable to view life from outside themselves. They are self-involved in their view of time as well, making organization skills difficult. At the end of the day, recalling a homework assignment from a first-period class in a seven-period day can be a major challenge. Providing a highly structured day and week with consistent routines and limiting passing periods with trips to lockers are methods for reducing students' confusion. Scheduling time so that students interact with only a few teachers each day, engaging in subject matter in one class that has obvious connections to that of other classes, and receiving homework for a limited number of classes promote development of organizational skills.

APPROPRIATE CURRICULUM AND INSTRUCTION

When classroom instruction improves, teachers may seek scheduling variations that further facilitate student growth. They may request more space, varied settings, shared planning time, and altered time periods. The responsibility of the principal is to encourage instructional growth, but this requires the ability to identify sound teaching practices. This section pinpoints some key components of effective instruction. The staff development section that follows addresses teaching activities that enhance interdisciplinary instruction, team teaching, and longer class periods.

Planning and Assessing

Envisioning what and how students are to achieve is a key component of effective teaching. Assessing and planning are two sides of the same coin. Assessing—(determining where you have been) and planning (deciding where you want to go and choosing the path to traverse in order to reach that destination)—lends power and purpose to educators (Glickman, Gordon, & Ross-Gordon, 1995). Research on teachers' planning shows that proactively planning activities not only increases teacher confidence, direction, and security but improves student learning as measured by test scores (Ubben & Hughes, 1992).

Providing adequate time for effective planning is one component of creating an instructionally driven schedule. Some key issues are time of day, who should share planning time, and length of planning period. Chapter 3 addresses planning periods in more detail.

Effective Teaching

In light of the overall school goals, teachers must first identify their particular classroom instructional goals and then decide which instructional models to emphasize. Over time, teachers should seek to increase their repertoire of models (Joyce & Weil, 1986). In a review of various instructional models, Joyce, Showers, and Rolheiser-Bennett (1987) identified those that have been found to most greatly influence student learning:

(1) Cooperative learning approaches represent what the authors term social models of teaching. They involve higher order thinking, problem solving, social skills, and social attitudes that have an effect on learning.

(2) Information-processing models include the use of advance organizers and mnemonics. (Mnemonics link letters of words with associated facts to be memorized).

(3) Synectics and nondirective teaching, which the authors term per-

sonal models of teaching, affect student achievement in basic areas, such as recall of information. (Synectics is a method for increasing students' creative capacity through deliberate use of metaphors and analogies.)

(4) Behavioral models which include mastery learning, direct instruction, and learning from simulations.

In a review of research on teaching, Ubben and Hughes (1992) point out that effective teachers use a variety of instructional methods rather than one.

Other sound practices applicable across models are explanation, discussion, inquiry, reading, role playing, demonstration, laboratory work, review, and use of homework. Teachers who use wait time, have high expectations for students, appropriately reinforce students, and frequently assess knowledge, also positively influence student success. Evaluation, though, must be continuous so that students are cognizant of errors as soon as possible (Hunter, 1987).

The time structure of the school day influences instruction. First, a teacher's choice of instructional activities is partially guided by the length of the class period. If periods are too short, cooperative learning, laboratory experiments requiring problem solving, and inquiry lessons may be limited or completely eliminated. Second, teachers often learn effective techniques from each other. Scheduling time when teachers can and must interact should positively influence instruction; for example, with teaming, teachers have a common planning period to work on instructional issues.

Teacher Behaviors and Instruction

Sergiovanni and Starratt (1993) discuss certain teacher behaviors that research has shown to be related to student gains on both criterion- and norm-reinforced tests. Advice to teachers includes the following (p. 108):

- establishing classroom rules that allow pupils to attend to personal and procedural needs without having to check with the teacher
- communicating expectations of high achievement
- starting each class by reviewing homework and by reviewing material covered in the previous few classes

- making the objectives of the new instructional episode clear to the students
- directly teaching the content or skill that will be measured on the test
- after teaching the new material, assessing student comprehension through questions and practice
- providing for uninterrupted successful practice that is not monitored by the teacher moving around the classroom
- maintaining direct engagement by the student on the academic task, engaged academic time being a critical variable for student achievement
- assigning homework to increase student familiarity with material
- holding review sessions weekly and monthly

Brophy (1992) adds to the list of teacher behaviors that make a difference in student achievement as measured by tests: emphasis on mastery, providing more opportunities to learn, managing classrooms well, and spending a great deal of time actively teaching students. Teachers can negatively influence student achievement as well: failing to provide adequate time for students to grasp a concept or practice a skill, ignoring personal interests or problems of students, and presenting material only through the lecture mode.

Many teacher behaviors are directly and indirectly related to the school day schedule. For example, class routines such as taking attendance are repetitive and time consuming when classes meet daily for short periods of time. Although teachers assign daily homework and conduct review sessions to improve student learning, students are often unable to cope with the complexities of completing assignments and differentiating among materials from seven or eight classes. Teachers unable to communicate with each other regularly may not be able to uniformly maintain classroom rules and high expectations for student achievement. Choices such as assigning a group of students to a particular team of teachers, lengthening the class period, and reducing the number of classes each day directly affect such scheduling issues.

The New Research on Teaching

Today, research stresses teaching in ways that students not only acquire a basic body of information that is stored and recalled but that they learn to create new knowledge by thinking, reasoning, and continuing to learn. Teachers must ask themselves if thinking skills should be taught in isolation, separate from the basic content, or whether to intertwine the two. Sergiovanni (1995) suggests,

> Taking the new research on teaching and learning seriously means making some changes in the way we have thought about organizing the classroom, planning for teaching, and arranging the curriculum. . . . As students become more involved in their own learning processes there will be more in-depth coverage of fewer topics. Learning will have to emphasize solving problems. (p. 192)

For teaching problem solving, the focus then moves from viewing instruction primarily in terms of how the teacher presents the material to including a focus on the activities students engage in individually or in groups. Teaching for problem solving requires tasks that are not easily bounded by specific time periods, place, or space.

Teaching techniques vary from school to school and teacher to teacher. The influence of time, however, is a common thread throughout. Of significance is the amount of time allowed for planning and teaching, the time of day and days of the week when a course is taught, the amount of time teachers have to interact with each other and with students, and the length of the school day. Throughout the scheduling process, the principal comes to terms with these factors.

STAFF DEVELOPMENT: A CHANGE ISSUE

Adopting a Sound Philosophy

Staff development implies personal and professional growth. Sergiovanni (1995) as well as Fullan (1991) reminds us that change takes place at two levels. Structural change, the first level, results in altered arrangements. Manipulating the schedule is an example of an altered arrangement. Change at the second level is normative and results in altered perspectives that, in turn, are likely to affect outcomes. "Normative change alters how teachers look at things, what they believe, what they want, what they know, and how they do things" (Sergiovanni & Starratt, 1993, p. 81). Lasting school improvement results from staff development that brings about normative change and should be the administrator's objective.

If normative change does not occur, staff development remains superficial. "Countless efforts at change are failing because they do not impact the culture of the school and the profession of teaching" (Fullan, 1991, p. 352). Elmore (1995) describes several studies of schools that had undergone extensive restructuring but where teachers failed to make any accompanying changes in how they taught, although the teachers were highly energized by their involvement in restructuring. Changes in how classes are scheduled accompanied by appropriate staff development is an example of linking normative and structural change. When scheduling changes result from altered beliefs regarding the school, new instructional approaches and increased student achievement are more predictable. Such change is accomplished through carefully planned staff development.

Normative change takes time. Fullan and Miles (1992) view change as a process, not an event. Time is needed to explain trust, to address the needs of those who are resisting, to involve all teachers, and to elicit parent and community support. As Sizer (1986) states, "Total school change does not imply radical, headlong speed, but rather attention to every aspect of the school" (p. 40) and suggests that schools should move forward at a very deliberate pace. In fact, gains may not be evident for several years. A study of block scheduling by Reid, Hierck, and Veregin (1994), examines gains in measures of achievement other than test scores; improvement was found to occur after the second year of the change. Three to five years may be required for meaningful staff development to greatly influence instruction and, consequently, student achievement.

With normative change as the ultimate goal, the school principal must begin planning for staff development by determining what is happening instructionally. How can a principal know if the effective teaching strategies just discussed are in place and what training needs exist? Glickman, Gordon, and Ross-Gordon (1995) suggest multiple ways of finding out: (a) eyes and ears (watching and asking), (b) records such as achievement tests, (c) third-party evaluation, (d) written open-ended teacher survey (e) check and ranking surveys in which teachers prioritize strengths and weaknesses of the school programs, (f) using the Delphi technique, a combination of open-ended survey and ranking, through a series of transmittals, and (g) employing nominal group techniques that ask teachers to not only assess their own instructional needs but set group goals. A combination of several of these should provide a clear picture of the needs. As well as improving classroom instruction, the needs assessment should reflect any organization change, such as moving to block scheduling or teaming.

The needs assessment is a base for forming and translating into practice visions and ideals for the school's instructional program. Staff development is the vehicle for that connection.

Characteristics of Effective Staff Development

In a study by Lawrence (as cited in Glickman, Gordon, & Ross-Gordon, 1995), ninety-seven studies and reports on successful staff development provide the basis for the following list of effective characteristics:

(1) Involvement of admininstrators and supervisors in planning and delivering the program
(2) Training experiences differentiated by teacher
(3) Placement of the teacher in an active role (generating materials, ideas, and behaviors)
(4) Emphasis on demonstrations, supervised trials and feedback, teacher sharing, and mutual assistance
(5) Linkage of activities to the general staff development program
(6) Teacher choice of goals and activities
(7) Teacher self-initiated and self-directed training activities

Loucks-Horsley and colleagues (as cited by Glickman, Gordon, & Ross-Gordon, 1995) also synthesized a set of characteristics of successful staff development programs that are commonly reported in the literature. These include the following:

(1) Collegiality and collaboration
(2) Experimentation and risk taking
(3) Incorporation of available knowledge bases
(4) Appropriate participant involvement in goal setting; implementation, evaluation, and decision making
(5) Time to work on staff development and assimilate new learnings
(6) Leadership and sustained administrative support
(7) Appropriate incentives and rewards
(8) Designs built on principles of adult learning and the change process

(9) Integration of individual goals with school and district goals
(10) Formal placement of the program within the philosophy and organizational structure of the school and district

Common themes are teacher involvement, experimentation, administrative support, links between staff development and other aspects of the school and district, and training that is directed toward teachers' needs. By following guidelines, the school staff prepares to assess the school day schedule, to evaluate alternatives, and to make choices appropriate to the students, school, and district.

Stages of Professional Development

Important to change, particularly to scheduling innovations, is the developmental level of the teachers. Sergiovanni and Starratt (1993) tie the content of training to teachers' developmental stages of professional growth. The first stage of growth, traditional in service, is directed at the first-year teacher. The focus is on job-related skills, training is delivered in short sessions, and content remains at the knowledge level. For example, the beginning teacher needs help making lesson plans, finding appropriate disciplinary techinques, and conducting parent conferences—training that experienced teachers no longer need.

The intermediate level of teacher growth is staff development. The assumption here is that teachers are professionals. Focus is on the development of professional expertise, and growth occurs through problem solving and inquiry. The primary responsibility for growth is shared by the supervisor and teacher, while content ranges around the comprehension and application levels. At this level, teachers, together with the principal, may explore alternate teaching methods to enhance student learning or closely examine individual students' instructional and personal needs.

The final level, renewal, is evident in staff members who view teaching as a vocation. Focus is on the development of personal and professional self, and change occurs through reflection and reevaluation and is highly self-directed with a minimum of supervisor involvement. Here, thinking and developing occur differently. For example, a teacher at this level may request learning styles or cooperative learning training, additional evaluation for self-improvement, or new teaching assignments. The principal may ask this teacher to conduct staff development, to become a mentor to new staff, or to explore innovative teaching techniques.

When considering scheduling formats, not only do individual teachers' levels of development need to be assessed but that of the faculty as a whole. For example, moving to arrangements as complicated as block scheduling or teaming when most of the staff is new would be difficult and could result in failure. On the other hand, if most teachers are at the renewal level and are able to engage in the type of analysis necessary for change, reform is more likely to be successful.

STAFF DEVELOPMENT AND SCHEDULING CHOICES

In many reports of schools undertaking new scheduling arrangements such as block scheduling or teaming, one issue that appears repeatedly is the need for training prior to and during the change process (Schroth & Dixon, 1996; Shortt & Thayer, 1995; Merenbloom, 1991). Guskey and Kifer (1995) conducted a thorough evaluation of the blocked restructuring program of one secondary school and found that the teachers reported a major disdvantage to be the need for considerable training and gleaning new ideas about teaching effectively in a 90-minute class period.

Several suggested first steps include visiting other campuses where change has been successfully implemented, researching all the alternative scheduling formats, and identifying major barriers. For some scheduling arrangements, training in some specific areas is particularly useful, and the following are suggested.

Block Scheduling

Any scheduling arrangement that includes longer or flexible periods of instruction requires training teachers to engage in strategies other than lecture, drill, and practice. Some that should be considered are

- cooperative learning training
- student assessment
- inductive learning
- methods that include manipulating, constructing, reconstructing, and experimenting
- social and group processing skills for students
- peer teaching

- development of learning centers
- seminar teaching

Teaming

Staff development initiatives for team teaching should focus on the issues that arise when a small group of students and teachers interact intensely with one another. Training should include

- team building
- goal setting and continuous goal assessment
- consensus building
- conflict resolution and problem-solving techniques
- cooperative learning
- team-teaching strategies
- interdisciplinary instruction
- development of thematic units with assessment

Any Scheduling Format

Whether traditional or nontraditional scheduling is the choice, most teachers need help learning to

- teach to a variety of learning styles
- teach higher-order thinking skills
- use problem-solving techniques with students
- use information-processing skills, such as advance organizers and mnemonics
- use technology in the classroom
- teach concept development and attainment
- manage their time

Principals should be aware that when teachers combine these strategies, there is greater potential for improving student achievement and for teachers to feel a sense of satisfaction with their work.

Having looked at what should be in place instructionally in every classroom and what training should occur before and during transition to new scheduling formats, we now take a closer look at the issue of change. Principals need to know how to go about making transitions so success of even seemingly minor improvement is increased. Knowing the pitfalls and barriers in advance allows a principal to plan for them rather than be caught off guard. The next chapter addresses these issues.

REFERENCES

Black, J. K., Puckett, M. B., & Bell, M. J. (1992). *The young child: Development from prebirth through age eight.* New York: Merrill Publishing Company.

Brophy, G. (1992). Probing the subtleties of subject-matter teaching. *Educational Leadership, 49*(7), 4–7.

Carnegie Council on Adolescent Development. (1989). *Turning points: Preparing American youth for the 21st century. The report of the task force on education of young adolescents.* New York: Carnegie Council on Adolescent Development.

Elmore, R. F. (1995). Structural reform and educational practice. *Educational Researcher, 24*(9), 23–26.

Fullan, M. G., & Miles, M. B. (1992). Getting reform right: What works and what doesn't. *Phi Delta Kappan, 73*(10), 745–752.

Fullan, M. G., & Stiegelbauer, S. (1991). *The new meaning of educational change.* New York: Teachers College Press.

George, P., & Lawrence, G. (1982). *A handbook for middle school teaching.* Glenview, IL: Scott, Foresman and Company.

Glickman, C. D., Gordon, S. P., & Ross-Gordon, J. M. (1995). *Supervision of instruction* (3rd ed.). Boston: Allyn & Bacon.

Guskey, T. R., & Kifer, E. (1995, April). *Evaluation of a high school block schedule restructuring program.* Paper presented at the annual meeting of the American Educational Research Association, San Francisco, CA.

Hunter, M. (1987). *Mastery teaching.* El Segundo, CA: TIP Publications.

Joyce, B., Showers, B., & Rolheiser-Bennett, C. (1987). Staff development and student learning: A synthesis of research on models of teaching. *Educational Leadership, 45*(2), 11–23.

Joyce, B., & Weil, M. (1986). *Models of teaching* (3rd ed.). Englewood Cliffs, NJ: Prentice Hall.

Kentta, B. (1993). The challenge of an integrated curriculum. *The School Administrator, 3*(50), 17–19.

Lorain, P. (1996). More than a scenery change: What it takes to move from junior highs to middle schools. *The School Administrator, 53*(6), 13–17.

Merenbloom, E. Y. (1991). *The team process.* Columbus, OH: National Middle School Association.

Pogrow, S. (1996). Reforming the wannabe reformers: Why education reforms almost always end up making things worse. *Phi Delta Kappan, 77*(10), 656–663.

Reid, W. M., Hierck, T., & Veregin, L. (1994). Measurable gains of block scheduling. *The School Administrator, 51*(3), 32–33.

Sarason, S. B. (1990). *The predictable failure of educational reform.* San Francisco, CA: Jossey-Bass Pub.

Schroth, G., & Dixon, J. (1996, October). The effects of block scheduling on student performance. *International Journal of Educational Reform, 5*(4), 472–476.

Schroth, G., & Dunbar, R. (1993, Fall). Mission Possible: One school's journey to site-based decision making. *Catalyst for Change, 24*(1), 24–26.

Sergiovanni, T. J. (1995). *The Principalship* (3rd ed.). Boston: Allyn & Bacon.

Sergiovanni, T. J., & Starratt, R. J. (1993). *Supervision: A redefinition.* New York: McGraw-Hill, Inc.

References

Shortt, T. L., & Thayer, Y. (1995, May). What can we expect to see in the next generation of block scheduling? *NASSP Bulletin, 79*(571), 53–65.

Sizer, T. R. (1986). Rebuilding: First steps by the Coalition of Essential Schools. *Phi Delta Kappan, 68*(1), 38–42.

Ubben, G. C., & Hughes, L. W. (1992). *The principal* (2nd ed.). Boston: Allyn & Bacon.

CHAPTER 2

Change

Nothing endures but change.
—Diogenes Laertius

INTRODUCTION

Effective leaders are capable of reframing the thinking of those whom they guide, enabling them to see that significant changes are not only imperative but achievable. Yet the challenges facing these leaders go beyond determining "what" needs to be done differently. They must also address "how" to execute these decisions in a manner that has the greatest possibility for success. Leaders must keep in mind that the accuracy of decisions alone can never compensate for poor implementation. (Conner, 1992, p. 9)

Schools are always involved in change. In fact, learning itself has been defined as change. It follows then, that schools, as "places of learning," are in reality "places of change." As educational leaders, principals must be knowledgeable about both the "what" and "how" of change. They must become operational and conceptual experts about such things as what changes are needed and who decides, how change happens (sources and processes), why some seemingly minor changes are needed and who decides, how change happens (sources and processes), why some seemingly positive changes don't happen while others do, how change can be led and managed, and strategies for helping self and others in coping with change. The purpose of this chapter is to acquaint

This chapter is authored by Anita Pankake.

readers with some general concepts regarding change and the change process. The information has been organized around three questions:

(1) What can be done to prepare for change?
(2) What can be expected when change occurs?
(3) What actions can help in preparing for change and in successfully managing the change process?

In the first section, "What can be done to prepare for change?" elements that help create a readiness for change are discussed. Some attitudes and behaviors are more helpful than others in this preparation process. Both people and the organizational context need to be ready if a smooth transition is to occur. Knowing some basic information about change and the change process can be significant in preparing for it. In the second section, some general statements are presented to capture some of the important assumptions and concepts of change and the change process. The statements are designed to be attention-getting and easy to remember. However, the information and explanations that follow the statements are included for a deeper appreciation of the concepts involved. Finally, the third section, "What actions can help in preparing for change and in successfully managing the change process?" offers some suggestions for action based on the information presented in the earlier sections. It is important to use knowledge about change and the change process in making decisions about what to change and how to make it happen.

The information presented here has general application to change and does not deal specifically with scheduling as a change. The intent of the generalizing is not to be evasive, but to be realistic. Good or bad, one of the interesting things about change and the change process is that it seems to be universal. That is, no matter the topic, nor where in the world it may be occurring, the basic elements of change and the change process are similar. According to Conner (1992), "the basic human reactions to change are the same in everyone." He adds, "Executives who successfully implement change, regardless of their location, display many of the same basic emotions, behaviors, and approaches" (p. 6). Similarly, Fullan (1991) notes that "any discussion with those involved in educational innovation and reform . . . quickly reveals that the nature of problems and many of the principles of success and failure have a great deal in common" (p. xiii). Additionally, he refers to the key feature in situations where change efforts have succeeded as "organized common sense."

In many ways, this makes learning about change and the change process a really productive activity. The information here can be useful in working with changes involving scheduling or any other aspect of the school. The information can be used as a framework for thinking and planning. The concepts have a sort of "one size fits all" nature. Conversely, it is also important to remember that every change effort needs to be shaped and molded to fit the uniquenesses of the specific place, time, and intent of the change being considered. While some aspects of change and the process of changing are universal, every change is unique. The balance between the generic and the unique is one that principals must strive to maintain if they are to become capable leaders and managers of change.

WHAT CAN BE DONE TO PREPARE FOR CHANGE?

Total preparation for change is not possible. No amount of planning and controlling can make the change process totally pedictable and surprise free. However, orchestrating some of the conditions in the organization can create a context for change that makes efforts more likely to persist and perhaps even succeed. Creating a readiness for change is an important task for principals. While there cannot be a 100% assurance of what will happen in a change effort, there can be a greater degree of assurance when leaders make a conscious effort to apply what is known about change and the process of changing and operate from some basic assumptions.

First, principals can prepare for change by assuming that change will happen. It is no longer an option to consider whether you do or don't want things to change; things *will* change. Things are changing all the time. As we move from the industrial age into the information age, changes are more rapid than ever. This environment of change will not only continue, but, the speed of change is likely to increase. Whether the changes being experienced are ones sought or ones thrust upon you really isn't the issue. The fact is, "Change is part of existing—we can't not change! . . . [It] will occur whether it is led or not" (Pankake, 1996, p. 27). However, if we do not choose the changes we desire and assess to be most important for the organization, we are allowing things to drift along and change by chance rather than plan. In either case, things will change. If principals can convince themselves and those with whom they work that change will happen, then a condition of readiness will be well under way. Making this proactive assumption will help develop what Conner (1992) calls "resilience" (the capacity to absorb a great deal of change with little or no demonstrated dysfunctional behavior). He claims resilience is what will determine who wins and who loses in the era of rapid change. Similarly, Pritchett (1996) asserts that if organizations are to succeed during the information age, individuals have to make it easier for the organization to change by becoming what he calls *world-class adapters.*

Another way principles can prepare for change is to make sure the proposed changes are needed and that those who will have to do the changing see the need and the benefits that changing will bring. These conditions are important for several reasons. First, desired changes do not happen unless there is a perceived need for them. As long as individuals and groups are satisfied with the way things are, little motivation to change exists. If change is to actually happen, those required to do the changing must see the need for it. As Kotter (1996) pointed out, "Major change is usually impossible unless most employees are willing to help, often to the point of making short-term sacrifices. But people will not make sacrifices, even if they are unhappy with the status quo, unless they think the potential benefits of change are attractive and unless they really believe that a transformation is possible" (p. 9).

If the individuals who actually have to implement the change do not see either the need for or the benefits of its implementation, the change has little chance of success. The benefits of changing may be obvious to the one who proposes it; however, they may not be so obvious to those who must make the change happen. Harvey (1990) suggests that the single most important question to be asked in any change effort may be "What's in it for the changee? What will he or she gain for the change effort?" (p. 58). He asserts that "if you seek success in your change efforts, you must examine the benefits—not to yourself, but to the changee" (p. 58). After all, not everyone views a proposed change as progress. Ordinarily, the one who proposes the change has determined why it is good and has already convinced himself or herself of the benefits to be accrued through implementation. However, it takes more than a proposal to make change happen. Those who must implement a change need information available to them that clearly points to the need for the change and identifies the personal as well as organizational benefits that will occur with its implementation.

A third condition that principals can create to get ready for change is clarity. According to James McGregor Burns (1978, cited in DuFour, 1991), the first thing a leader must do to influence others to clarify his or her own goals" (p. 15). Principals need to be clear about what is to change and what things will be like when it is successfully implemented. Such clarity is essential first for the leader and then for those who are to follow; clarity requires articulating a picture of the future. According to Fullan (1991), "Clarity (about goals and means) is a perennial problem in the change process. Even when there is agreement that some kind of change is needed . . . the adopted change may not be at all clear about what teachers should do differently . . . the more complex the reform . . . the greater the problem of clarity" (p. 70). Harvey (1990) emphasized that "too often change efforts fail because members of a group make different presumptions about what they want to accomplish." He says one common assumption is that everyone knows what is meant when, most likely, they do not. His solution is "to describe the change effort in one short, clear paragraph" (p. 52). If that cannot be done, more thought and analysis are necessary before initiating the change.

Once what is to change is known and has been clearly described, principals need to determine if the skills needed to achieve the future state exist or if training to secure these skills will be required. According to Miles and Louis (1990), skill is often ignored. They assert that, just because you know that something can help or is workable in a situation, it does not mean you know how to do it. Merely wanting to and knowing what it is that could or should be done is quite different from knowing how to make it happen. They also admonish that learning skills extend beyond listening and watching. Training and development may require actually practicing the skill and receiving feedback in order to refine and reshape the new behavior. In other words, training and development should come in a variety of formats. These can range from the well-known "sit and get" sessions to individualized on-the-job coaching or collaborative study groups for long-term organizational improvement. According to Sparks and Loucks-Horsley (1990), "Staff development is defined as those processes that improve the job-related knowledge, skills, or attitudes of school employees . . ." (p. 6). Fullan (1990) points out that "successful change involves learning how to do something new. As such, the process of implementation is essentially a learning process" (p. 4). He adds that "staff development should be innovation-related, continuous during the course of implementation and involve a variety of formal . . . and informal . . . components" (p. 4). While training and development are needed early in the change process, adequate training and development components later on are important as well. Additionally, the nonlinear, multifaceted process of change may well require that a range of training and development components occur simultaneously.

Implementation is essentially a learning process (Fullan, 1991), and learning requires change. Thus, an important aspect of being ready for change is to understand that training and development must be continuous, relevant, and timely. Pritchett's (1996) recommendations for achieving success in the information age state that "our thinking should be centered on building our knowledge base." To do this, he suggested that everyone in the organization "make space in our daily schedules to be 'in school,'" that is, everyone needs "daily study time" just to keep up. There will be no beginning or end to the training and development needed to change because there will be no end to changing; knowing this and acting appropriately is a state of readiness that will position your organization to be more likely to succeed as change efforts get under way.

A fifth condition that principals can create to prepare for change is to secure the resources (time, energy, money, etc.) and long-term commitment for the change. Securing resources and gaining long-term commitment travel hand-in-hand. Too often in change projects, resources (in varying forms) are committed to the project in its early stages. But, as the newness wears off, other change initiatives appear on the agenda, leadership changes occur, and myriad other distractions materialize, so the resources for the change get reallocated to other projects. The assumption is made that only "start-up" demands resources and somehow maintenance requires none. Most of us know that nothing could be farther from the truth. In fact, in some situations, the start-up costs are minimal compared to the cost of upkeep! According to Miles and Louis (1990), "One of the biggest issues is facing up to the fact that changes cost money. . . . Finding and getting resources takes tenacity—hanging in there and persisting against obstacles" (p. 59).

Additionally, it is important for everyone to realize that not all the costs of change can be measured with money. Certainly, money can buy many of the items needed for change to succeed. However, money cannot secure all of the costs. The costs for change can be time or energy, the loss of a valued colleague, a move from one place to another, the loss of a comfortable routine, loss of position of status, or a need to develop new relationships.

> Change involves giving up some things to get some other things — hopefully new and improved. . . . The most important cost to recognize is what it costs an individual to move from the known to the unknown. . . . Because change happens one person at a time, the cost of losing the known is a very individual matter. . . . Leaders need to work with individuals to help each person see the costs-benefits for them in changing. The costs of losing the known is the price that must be paid for changing. (Pankake, 1996, p. 26)

In addition to securing resources and being sensitive to individual costs, commitment to stay the course in terms of time is necessary if change efforts are to succeed. With the general estimate of three to five years for any substantive change to occur, the leader of the change must be ready to commit for the long-term. This aligns with the oft heard "change is a process, not an event" (Fullan, 1991; Hord et al., 1987). "Treating change as an event is a sure way to reduce the possibilities of success" (Pankake, 1996, p. 25).

Finally, the level of success that change efforts have experienced in the past will be a good indication of what may be predicted in the next effort. Principals are encouraged to spend some time analyzing the success record of previous efforts to change. This can be helpful in planning for the current effort. As the old saying goes, "Success breeds success," and it seems to be as true with change as with anything else. If the organization has sucessfully implemented changes in the past, the same is likely to be true about future efforts. Conversely, if the history of the organization is one of failed efforts with various change projects, then, that too is likely to be the pattern in the future. An organization with a dismal track record of change efforts needs to be careful in selecting strategies for introducing new efforts. Literally building a history of success will be necessary in reversing the anticipation of failure that has built up in the past. Taking small, positive steps and being sure to celebrate each positive step as a victory will help to develop a positive, self-fulfilling prophecy of success. Decisions about what changes to pursue will be critical (even more than they usually are), and pacing will be less concerned with speed and more with continuous progress. Miles and Louis (1990) also made an issue of "will" in their work with change in urban high schools. They identified "will" as "coming in part from success experiences and in part from a context or environment which encourages change efforts, both of which lead people to believe that their actions can make a difference" (p. 58).

Reinforcing that readiness for change is a condition of degree rather than an absolute. Even if principals act on all the information noted here, a guarantee that change will be welcomed with enthusiasm and implemented smoothly is not ensured. However, things are more likely to start off with optimism for success if principals will

- develop a mind-set that assumes change will happen
- make sure the proposed changes are needed and will produce benefits
- be clear about what is to change and share their vision of the future with others
- secure the resources (time, energy, money, etc.) and make a long-term commitment for the change
- determine what skills are needed and secure appropriate training
- spend time analyzing the success of previous efforts to change in order to determine best strategies for current efforts

Getting ready for change is important, but as the history of educational change has chronicled, many, if not most, initiations fail the test of successful implementation. There is more to change than just getting started. Knowing what to expect once implementation gets under way is equally important.

WHAT TO EXPECT WHEN CHANGE OCCURS

Spending some time on what to expect when change occurs may assist principals in a number of ways. First, the amount of time lost in getting over surprise and disappointment may be reduced. Additionally, planning what to do, when to do it, how, and why may be expedited. Ten generalizations have been identified here. Each is stated and followed by some additional information to give it meaning. For starters, when change occurs, principals can expect

(1) Less than orderly progression
(2) Resistance in varying degrees and for lots of reasons
(3) Alternating periods of ambiguity and clarity
(4) Rejection if the change isn't useful and usable
(5) Variation in enthusiasm and momentum over time
(6) Additional changes to be required

(7) Continuing time requirements
(8) Atrophy without attention
(9) Continuing and perhaps even increasing resource needs
(10) Some anticipated and some unanticipated results.

(1) When change occurs, principals can expect the process to follow a less than orderly progression. Generally, three phases are identified in the change process, i.e., initiation, implementation, and institutionalization or continuation. Figures depicting these change phases often show a neat, linear progression from initiation to implementation to institutionalization. In reality, the progression is not so neat and linear as the figures imply. In reality, the progress of change might better be depicted as several turns of a kaleidoscope lens or a performance of a skilled juggler. In any case, the result is alternating levels (degrees) of clarity and ambiguity, shifts from initiating to implementing some parts of the change while simultaneously moving back to initiating for other aspects of the change. Also, as some elements of one change project are being institutionalized, another change project may just be initiated! Kotter (1996) indicates that, "major change initiatives are made up of a number of smaller projects that also tend to go through the multi-step process. So at any one time, you might be halfway through the overall effort, finished with a few of the smaller pieces, and just beginning other projects. The net effect is like wheels within wheels" (p. 24). In other words, change is "nonlinear, multi-faceted and a mess in the middle" (Pankake, 1996, p. 26).

(2) When change occurs, principals can expect that resistance will occur in varying degrees and for a variety of reasons. If you can count on anything in the change process, it is resistance. People resist changes for all kinds of reasons—none of which have to make sense to anyone except the person who is resisting. Resistance to change rarely stems from some kind of spite or belligerence but is more likely to be from fear of the unknown, loss of security, organizational constraints, bureaucratic dysfunction, differences in philosophy or logic, or even from concern for a flawed planning or analysis of need. Harvey (1990) refers to resistance as being natural and reasonable until the individual is able to see the "pay-off," i.e., benefits, in changing. In a recent speech, Fullan (1996) noted that "every act of resistance has an element of good sense." Not everyone will be in favor of the change (whatever it is). This particular aspect of change seems to be one that, even when we know and understand it, never ceases to amaze us when it occurs.

It does not make any difference what the change is; someone will be against it for some reason. Most changes initiated in schools and/or to schools have the intent of making things better. The problem, of course, is that what one individual perceives as better or an improvement may be perceived by someone else as a step backward or perhaps even useless. Rather than view those who express resistance as "the bad guys" and those who accept without question as the "good guys," principals would benefit from using resistance as feedback and opportunity for improving the change process. Striking a balance between countering the resistor and learning from them is important for principals to achieve. What principals want to be sure to avoid is ignoring resistance. For one thing, ignoring concerns expressed by those you want to persuade to follow you is "leadership suicide." Additionally, expressions of resistance may have important information that can be used to avoid problems during implementation; or perhaps, new perspectives can be ascertained so that planning can be more comprehensive, especially as regards various consequences of actions taken. Myriad possibilities exist; all of them can enhance the quality of thinking about change and implementing the process of changing. Principals should use resistance as an opportunity for improvement and learning rather than actions to be stopped.

(3) When change occurs, principals can expect alternating periods of ambiguity and clarity. While clarity was recommended as essential for getting ready for change, clarity can be persistent in the long-term but fleeting in the short-term. The alternating periods of ambiguity and clarity can be likened to what happens when driving in fog. It is clear in your mind where you are heading; however, the journey itself literally unfolds or becomes clear a little bit at a time. That which is directly ahead, the immediate future, has some clarity, while other images that are at a distance are more vague and indistinguishable, perhaps even unseen. Along these lines, Fullan (1991) asserts that "clarification is likely to come in large part through practice" (p. 106). He notes further, "Significant change involves a certain amount of ambiguity, ambivalence, and uncertainty for the individual about the meaning of the change. Thus, effective implementation is a *process of clarification*" (p. 106).

(4) When change occurs, principals can expect rejection if the change is not useful and usable. While this rejection may not be overt, it will happen. If the initiated change cannot be understood by teachers (or anyone else who has to use it) and it does not fit into the reality of

their daily existence, then it will be rejected. Doyle and Ponder (1977–78, cited in Fullan, 1991) identified a concept they named the "practicality ethic." The concept involved such things as teachers' assessments of how well students would respond to an innovation, how clear the processes of implementation were defined, and the balance of personal and professional investments to the benefits received. More recently, Pankake and Palmer (1996) found this concept still active in their study of inclusion. They concluded that "what is practical and of immediate use is the most helpful to teachers trying to implement change" (p. 29). Teachers and other school personnel have more than enough to keep them busy. Unless the changes proposed are helpful, easily understandable, and fit in with most of what is already happening, the individuals are unlikely to invest the time, energy, patience, and persistance needed to implement it.

(5) When change occurs, principals can expect a variation in enthusiasm and momentum over time. Even those who are in favor of the proposed change will vary in levels of enthusiasm, commitment, and willingness to start. It is important for principals to recognize and work within this reality. This may be the most important aspect for principals to know, especially as implementation gets under way. There is a phenomenon knows as the "implementation dip," which is bound to occur when things do not go as smoothly as planned or perhaps do not go at all. During these times, even the staunch supporters of the particular change will experience doubt and perhaps even withdraw support. Believe it or not, even principals will experience such times. These times are less likely to occur, or at least be less severe, if the clarity issue has been tended to in the readiness stages noted earlier as part of getting ready for change. Again, however, the important thing is to know this will happen and may even happen to you. Persistence and patience are two important characteristics to employ during these times. Additionally, planning celebrations of the achievements thus far can help individuals recall why this change was undertaken, how much progress has been made, and why it is important to keep working at getting the change accomplished. Rather than initiate changes that may sound good but never make it to regular use in the classrooms of the schools, Pogrow (1996) asserts that "the most important changes are incremental ones" (p. 659) and the "reform requires technology, methodology, structure, dosages, and materials" (p. 658).

(6) When change occurs, principals can expect additional changes to be required. As changes occur, they will require changes in the people,

processes, and the context. As Rifkin (1980) expressed in this fascinating work, *Entropy,* "Everything in this world is connected with everything else in a delicate and complex web of interrelationships" (p. 226). Not unlike Boyd's (1992) assertion regarding the concept of systemic, everything is connected to everything. As people change and gain new skills and attitudes, various processes will undergo changes; it may also be the case that some of the new behaviors, or beliefs, or processes will require that the organizational context change. New policies may need to be created. Certainly, the alignment of policies will need to be checked as things change. Sometimes policies that were adequate for one situation will be obstructive as new situations emerge. An example of this is the statement found in the report from the National Commission on Teaching and America's Future, *What Matters Most:* "Most schools and teachers cannot produce the kind of learning demanded by the new reform . . . not because they do not want to, but because they do not know how, and the systems in which they work do not support them in doing so" (cited in Richardson, 1996, p. 1). The larger organization must be changed to accommodate changes being made in various parts of the organization. If schedules are changed then staffing, course offerings, teaching strategies, evaluation procedures, grading, room assignments, etc., may also require changes or become barriers to the effort. Resistance can come from the organization itself as well as any individual in it. Hord (1995) writes about "creating a context for change" (p. 1). And Boyd (1992) notes that "Regardless of the new program or changes a school wishes to initiate, those leading school improvement efforts need an understanding of the complex nature of the school prior to and during the change effort in order to sustain implementation" (p. 10).

(7) When change occurs, principals can expect continuing time requirements for progress to become evident. The change literature is pretty clear that three to five years is minimal for even a moderately complex change to make substantial change. In fact, seven to ten years from initiation to full institutionalization is even more likely, particularly if major restructuring efforts are under way (Fullan, 1991). This recognition of the need for time provides the basis for the often heard admonishment that "change is a process, not an event" (for example see Fullan, 1991; Hord et al., 1987). It is important to realize also that the time change takes is most often referenced in terms of years. However, those years are made up of minutes, hours, days, weeks, and months. If these minutes, hours, days, weeks, and months are not focused on

efforts to bring this change to reality, the years will come and go, and the changes will be a list of things we were going to do or things we started but didn't finish. It is the time that is taken every day that adds up to the power of the three to five years for change to happen. Harvey (1990) said it well in stating, "We must recognize that change does not occur all at once. Change comes in stages" (p. 25). While he recognizes the typical three to five year interval, he recommends that a single year is the best base for planning. He asserts that the single-year planning mechanism is manageable and allows a reformulation of needed strategies at the end of that time period.

(8) When change occurs, principals can expect atrophy without attention. If it isn't monitored, it probably won't happen. DuFour (1991) referred to monitoring as paying attention. If we are sincere in wanting something to succeed, we will pay attention to it — not just to get it started, but throughout its existence. We apply this idea to a variety of aspects of life, e.g., child-rearing, edible cooking, good health, reliable transportation, a fruitful garden, etc. All of these activities take time and attention to start, but they also require monitoring as making them happen gets under way. For example, the attention and care of infants is essential to child-rearing; however, children require attention and care at every stage of their development. Parents who continue to monitor their children's development, making adjustments as needed, are more likely to see the development go more smoothly. The purchase of a new automobile will provide reliable transportation initially, but over the long-term, attention must be paid to maintenance. The new car that is not monitored through regular maintenance will soon become unreliable. And finally, the garden that is plowed and planted in the spring but never weeded, watered, or fertilized throughout the growing season will produce only by chance.

Advocacy is important to the success of the change process, and monitoring is one of the most powerful means of advocating a change. This is a variation of the old saying about people paying attention to what gets measured. With change, one of the measures people will use to determine whether they should pursue a change or not is how much attention is paid to that change by the leadership, i.e., the principal. If it soon slips off the principal's priority list, it will slip off everyone else's list as well. Harvey (1990) asserted that "change plans will falter unless there is a system for monitoring implementation of action plans and their effectiveness in reaching the desired point" (p. 84).

(9) When change occurs, principals can expect continuing and per-

haps even increasing resource needs. Recall that in getting ready for change, securing resources and long-term commitment were identified as elements that help create the condition of readiness for change. As implementation gets under way, that need will become even more evident. Costs may increase as the change moves to implementation. For example, the cost of release time for teachers involved in the pilot project for interdisciplinary teaming is minimal compared to the cost of release time for all teachers to work in such teaming situations. The initial costs of technology installation will be minimal compared to the costs of what is needed as individuals become more literate in technology and find more and more uses for it, require more sophisticated software, and look for more and more powerful and current hardware. While these resources may not necessarily need to be new resources, they must come from somewhere. Reallocating existing resources can be done, but will be viewed by those who "lose" those resources as one of the "costs" of change—which they may or may not pay willingly. Fullan and Miles (1992) noted that "change is resource-hungry" (p. 750). As change gets under way, resources in all forms will be needed if implementation is to succeed and principals can expect to be viewed as a resource provider.

(10) When change occurs, principals can expect some anticipated and some unexpected results. This relates closely to the philosophy that change follows a less than linear progression. While change can be planned and plans for implementation can be developed, what will happen during the change process is impossible to totally predict. One of the reasons for this is the interconnectedness of everything. While the term is used frequently in literature and conversations about change, the meaning of interconnectedness may not be as clearly understood as it would seem from its frequent use. As Rifkin (1980) pointed out, "Everything in this world is connected with everything else in a delicate and complex web of interrelationships" (p. 226). This is reinforced in Fullan's (1993) assertion regarding increasing our skills in working with change, i.e., "The goal then is to get into the habit of experiencing and thinking about educational change processes as an overlapping series of dynamically complex phenomena" (p. 21).

Realizing this interconnected complexity of the various systems and subsystems in which schools exist is important to helping us overcome surprise and disappointment when a change in one part of the school requires or results in changes in other parts of the system. Change brings consequences, opportunities, and new proposals and vice versa, i.e., "Take any educational policy or problem and start listing all the forces that could figure in the solution and that would need to be influenced to make for productive change . . . realize that every new variable that enters the equation—those unpredictable but inevitable noise factors—produce ten other ramifications, which in turn produces tens of other reactions and on and on" (Fullan, 1993, p. 19). Some of the required and/or resulting changes are anticipated; many are not. Some of these changes bring about new opportunities, and others require that current (sometimes popular) activities be abondoned. For too long, change in schools has been planned as if it existed in some sort of isolation, apart from anything else inside or outside the school. This is far from reality, and principals must cease thinking and leading as if this were true. Rather, the reality of the systemic nature of change needs not only to be voiced but also to be observed.

These ten responses to the question "What can principals expect when change occurs?" are by no means exhaustive. Each of them is connected to all of the others and to other concepts that have not even been identified in this chapter. These ten, in fact, should be thought of as a primer in a comprehensive program of learning about change and the change process.

WHAT ACTIONS CAN HELP IN PREPARING FOR CHANGE AND IN SUCCESSFULLY MANAGING THE CHANGE PROCESS?

The strategies suggested here are based on concepts presented in the previous sections. These are by no means the only strategies that can be generated from this information or that can be derived from other information about change and the change process. Readers are encouraged to use the information to think through the individual situations they face and seek ways to apply the knowledge gleaned.

Actions That Help in Preparing for Change

- Attend workshops and read professional journals to stay aware of initiatives within the profession.
- Monitor political and social initiatives at the local (including school board meetings), state, and national levels.
- Visit with some local business leaders to discuss trends.

- Draw a "change timeline" for your own life (ask others in the organization to do the same for their own lives) to create a visual representation of the continuous changes in your and their experience.
- Gather data that demonstrate there is a problem and that the proposed change will solve (or help solve) the problem.
- Disseminate this information to all parties involved.
- Invite representatives who have implemented the proposed change in their organization to talk with individuals in your organization about how the change has benefited them.
- Beware of the same stuff in a new package and/or a new package for the same stuff.
- Involve those who must implement the change in identifying problems and generating possible solutions for them.
- Put the proposed change in writing, and have others read it.
- Administer the Stages of Concern Questionnaire (SoCQ) Hord et al., 1987) to help identify the kinds of needs participants have regarding the change.
- Ask participants to do a self-assessment of knowledge and skill levels related to the proposed change.
- Interview individuals who have implemented the same or similar change regarding needed skills.
- Consult an external agency or consultant with expertise regarding knowledge and skills related to the innovation to ask for assistance in both the assessment and development of needed skills.
- Ask for resources.
- Reallocate resources to the new effort from an unproductive outlived project.
- Apply for a grant (multi-year, if possible).
- Identify items that are not being used, and barter with others in the school or district to secure what you need.
- Reorganize schedules to accrue time.
- Develop a partnership with a local university or business to obtain student helpers and volunteers.
- Do a presentation on the proposed change for the school board.
- Write the change into a multiple-year improvement plan.
- Involve a variety of groups in the planning.
- Find a central office advocate for the change.

- Do a timeline of the change efforts in this organization over the past three to five years, adding as much detail as possible regarding what the change was, why it was proposed, by whom, what training was done, etc., for each of the changes noted on the timeline.
- Interview some of the veteran staff in the school about change efforts in the past asking them to talk freely about what went well and what went wrong in those efforts.
- Sort and categorize the information gathered, looking for themes and patterns to determine what went well and what created problems or barriers in the change efforts.

The strategies proposed thus far are related to those conditions identified as helpful in getting ready for change. Ten responses to the question "What can be expected when change occurs?" were offered in the second part of the chapter. The strategies offered next are based on these ten responses.

Actions to Help in Successfully Managing the Change Process

- Communicate often and in a variety of formats, i.e., talk, talk, talk, and listen, listen, listen!
- Provide opportunities to ask questions, provide information, request suggestions for improvement, and otherwise allow individuals to give and get information at regular intervals as the change is implemented.
- Build in time for everyone to process—individually and in groups—about how the change is going and how things might be improved.
- Arrange meetings for those with implementation responsibilities so they can encourage and help each other in their efforts to persist in changing.
- Listen to and learn from both resistors and advocates.
- Gather feedback often and in a variety of ways, such as group sessions, individual sessions/interviews, through representatives [such as Bridges (1991) Transition Monitoring Team], through written surveys or through debriefing sessions using external consultants.
- Try to find out why individuals or groups are resisting.

- Use feedback to evaluate and improve the proposed change and the implementation process.
- Expect and even plan for simultaneous/overlapping activities, as well as sequenced activities regarding what may/will happen during any particular change effort.
- Plan using circles, webs, and picture maps.
- Provide support continuously and in the necessary forms.
- Include the practical content of training early in the effort, and focus on conceptual information later.
- Offer feedback to everyone, even those who seem to be having little if any trouble.
- Allow everyone to offer their own feedback on how things are going and what might be done to improve them.
- Train those who will be leading and facilitating the change efforts.
- Balance when training is provided so that important information and skills are not given too soon nor too late to be useful to those who need them.
- Personalize training and development as much as possible—one size does not fill all when it comes to professional training and development for change.
- Administer the SoCQ (Hord et al., 1989) periodically, and monitor the movement or lack thereof through the concerns profile.
- Use the information to determine what support to provide.
- Take walks throughout the building observing what is or isn't going on that relates to the change effort's success.
- Conduct periodic celebrations of the achievements toward implementation.
- Ask individuals and/or groups of participants to give the periodic reports on their progress to the rest of the staff.
- Look everywhere for resources, and think of everything as a resource.
- Avoid starting too many changes at one time; this creates change overload.
- Plan for a series of short-term successes.
- Form study groups to learn more about a particular program or topic.

Finally, principals and other school leaders are encouraged to continue to read about and attend workshops focused on change and the change process. Continuing to learn is a responsibility of leadership. Additional information is available, and more is being discovered every day; no doubt the most important skill in learning to lead and manage change is to become a life-long learner in all capacities. Setting the model for continuous learning, asking the "I wonder" questions that serve as the catalysts to inquiries of importance, and offering an honest "I don't know, but I'll see what I can find out" when appropriate are powerful strategies for principals and teachers to develop as leaders and managers of change.

REFERENCES

Boyd, V. (1992). *School context: Bridge or barrier to change?* Austin, TX: Southwest Educational Development Laboratory.
Bridges, W. (1991). *Managing transitions: Making the most of change.* Reading, MA: Addison-Wesley.
Conner, D. R. (1992). *Managing at the speed of change: How resilient managers succeed and prosper when others fail.* New York: Villard Books.
DuFour, R. P. (1991). *The principal as staff developer.* Bloomington, IN: National Education Service.
Fullan, M. G. (1990). Staff development, innovation and institutional development. In B. Joyce (Ed.) *Changing school culture through staff development* (pp. 3–25). Alexandria, VA: Association for Supervision and Curriculum Development.
Fullan, M., & Stiegelbauer, S. (1991). *The new meaning of educational change* (2nd ed.). New York: Teachers College Press, Columbia University.
Fullan, M. (1993). *Change forces: Probing the depths of educational reform.* New York: The Falmer Press.
Fullan, M. (December, 1996). *School change: What's worth fighting for out there.* Distinguished Lecture Series, 28th Annual Conference of the National Staff Development Council, Vancouver, British Columbia.
Fullan, M. G., & Miles, M. B. (1992). Getting reform right: What works and what doesn't. *Phi Delta Kappan, 73*(10), 745–751.
Harvey, T. R. (1990). *Checklist for change: A pragmatic approach to creating and controlling change.* Boston: Allyn & Bacon.
Hord, S. M., Rutherford, W. L., Huling-Austin, L. & Hall, G. E. (1987). *Taking charge of change.* Alexandria, VA: Association for Supervision and Curriculum Development.
Hord, S. (1995). *Change processes: Creating a content for change—Issue II.* Austin, TX: Texas Association for Supervision and Curriculum Development.
Kotter, J. P. (1996). *Leading change.* Boston, MA: Harvard Business School Press.
Miles, M. B., & Louis, K. S. (1990). Mustering the will and skill for change. *Educational Leadership, 47* (8), 57–61.
Pankake, A. M. (1996). Change and technology leadership: Two sides of the same coin. *Educational Considerations, 23*(2), 25–28.

Pankake, A. M., & Palmer, B. (1996). Making the connections: Linking staff development interventions to implementation of full inclusion. *Journal of Staff Development, 17*(3), 26–30.

Pogrow, S. (1996). Reforming the wannabe reformer: Why education reforms almost always end up making things worse. *Phi Delta Kappan, 77*(10), 656–663.

Pritchett, P. (1996). *Mindshift,* Dallas, TX: Pritchett & Associates.

Richardson, J. (1996, Nov.). Teacher knowledge, skills most important influences on student learning. *The Developer,* Oxford, OH: National Staff Development Council.

Rifkin, J., & Howard, J. (1980). *Entropy: A new world view.* New York: The Viking Press.

Sparks, D., & Loucks-Horsley, S. (1990). *Five models of staff development for teachers.* Oxford, OH: National Staff Development Council.

CHAPTER 3

Meeting Challenges, Facing Problems

The shoe that fits one person pinches another; there is no recipe for living that suits all cases. Each of us carries his own life-form—an indeterminable form which cannot be superseded by any other.
—Carl Jung (1933)

The new principal needs information about the school and its environment in order to create a schedule that best services the institution's stated goals and objectives. This chapter first addresses considerations that inherently accompany scheduling, a discussion that should heighten the new principal's awareness of the pervasive nature of scheduling. Additional considerations unique to block scheduling and teaming follow. Finally, definitions and analyses of traditional, block, and team scheduling and their variations should aid those considering teaming or block scheduling. Those who decide to go forward will be aware of the crucial adjustments they may anticipate. Others will clearly see that a change is not in order and decide to enhance the current schedule or move forward in small steps.

Throughout this chapter, it will become clear that scheduling requires a multitude of judgments, some more complex than others. For example, determinations about budget and space are fairly clear. Less concrete, and consequently more difficult, is discerning teachers' and parents' attitudes about course offerings and assignment of students to classes. Moving forward from this point requires the principal to examine each piece of the scheduling puzzle and either adopt, discard, or subject it to further scrutiny.

First are considerations that are generic to all types of scheduling models, followed by those of particular interest to schools contemplating either block scheduling, teaming, or both. Within these two categories, topics are (1) student issues, (2) teacher considerations, and (3) other, related matters.

CONSIDERATIONS FOR ALL SCHEDULING MODELS

No matter how students are scheduled into classes and no matter how long those classes last, some issues inherently accompany decisions regarding the configuration of the school day.

Students

STUDENT POPULATION

The following types of questions about student populations open the needs assessment. Are student achievement scores generally low, and, when the data are disaggregated, do some student populations have lower scores than others? Does the school have a large population of high achieving students? What are the goals of students; are they mostly college bound or are most interested in a trade? These questions influence course offerings, assignments, the amount of time students spend studying each particular subject, and guidelines for grouping. Schools with large numbers of low achieving students may increase the time and size of math classes to improve achievement. Other schools wisely offer a wide variety of advanced courses to stimulate the interest of large groups of honors level students. If an analysis shows that a particular subgroup of students is deficient in an area, it may be important to include tutoring classes within the school day.

ABILITY GROUPING

The principal and staff must evaluate ability grouping, or tracking, because many scheduling decisions surround this issue. Changing in-class grouping is common at the elementary level, because teachers readily move students from one level to another when students progress. While most traditional middle and junior high schools also ability group students, they do so by entire classes, for example, high, middle, and low level classes (McPartland, 1989). The issue of tracking has taken higher priority over the last decade as one goal of the middle school movement, influenced by *Turning Points* is to reduce and even eliminate ability grouping (Carnegie Council on Adolescent Development, 1989).

Every scheduling decision has major implications. Decisions about how many levels to create, according to which criteria, and for which subjects are critical. Teachers generally have strong feelings about which levels they are assigned to teach and can become overburdened and disgruntled if directed to teach a large number of lower achieving students. Teachers with longer tenure sometimes have vested interest in teaching higher level classes and feel their reward for years of service is continued assignment to those courses (Canady & Rettig, 1992). The master schedule must offer classes for every level, at various times of the day to accommodate all students. Certainly, the absence of grouping makes creating a master schedule infinitely easier. Ubben and Hughes (1992) offer the following guidelines for student placement:

(1) For purposes of assigning students to individual teachers or teams, a heterogeneous or mixed grouping plan is usually best.
(2) Homogeneous grouping should take place in the classroom and should be done by teachers. The basis for internal class grouping can be interest, achievement, skill, age, or designed heterogeneity.
(3) Homogeneous grouping should be flexible with several different grouping patterns used each day. All homogeneous groups are usually of short duration. Flexibility is necessary because of the changing nature of groups and the problems of negative student self-concept or poor teacher attitudes that can develop from rigid homogeneous grouping patterns.
(4) Homogeneous groups should not be used for more than one-third of each school day. (p. 220)

STUDENT BEHAVIOR

Do teachers place discipline as a high priority for school improvement? Do parents complain frequently about student behavior? How does the community view the climate of the school? If discipline is a major concern that needs to be addressed by more than tightening rules and regulations, the following merit consideration: (a) reduce the number of times in the day students go to their lockers, (b) carefully make assignments so problematic students are not scheduled together, (c) limit the size and length of classes, (d) arrange class locations so that distance traveled between classes is as short as possible, (e) build detention time into the school day, e.g., at lunch, and (f) assign particular teachers primary responsibility for each student. Some schools extend the first or last period of the day to include additional time for homeroom for routine housekeeping matters and where teachers give personal attention to students. This can include calling parents, making sure homework assignments are in order, and solving individual problems. These interventions alone will not solve a problem so pervasive as chronic disruptive behavior but will provide support for other programs.

SPECIAL EDUCATION STUDENTS

As schools are increasingly encouraged to include students with disabilities in regular classrooms, special education teachers and aides spend much of their time helping students function in mainstreamed settings. How will students with disabilities be assigned to classes? What schedule best uses special education staff time? Which disabled students' needs best match certain teachers' strengths? For example, an emotionally disturbed student needs to be in a highly structured classroom and at a time when special education staff is available. A student with social problems will benefit from a teacher using cooperative learning techniques. How many special students should work with any one teacher? Overburdening a master teacher who has the ability to handle difficult students creates morale problems. Distributing special students equally among faculty creates other problems if teachers and students do not get along. Admission, review, and dismissal meetings require administrative input, making placement in special education necessarily formal.

Teachers

PLANNING PERIODS

When will each teacher have planning time? Will the administrator consider teacher requests? Will a teacher who did not receive her preference the previous year have priority this year? Will planning periods be rotated so that no one teacher or grade receives the same time for planning each year? Will subject area teams share planning periods? For example, will all science teachers have fifth period for planning? Will teaming teachers have both the shared period and one for individual planning? Planning periods impact teachers' daily lives so they usually have preferences. Some want release time early, others prefer the middle of the day, and still others choose late periods; some want to share planning time with their friends or teammates. Elementary school teachers often request late afternoon, thinking that core subjects such as reading are best taught early in the day when both they and the students are fresh. Full-day kindergarten teachers like to have students work in the morning, nap after lunch, and receive physical education during teachers' planning time at the end of the day. Planning periods for itinerant teachers and specialists may abut travel time; special programs directors often dictate schedules. A principal must work around these situations in designing the schedule, whatever the model. Sharing the decision with teachers will prevent problems at a later time.

TEACHER PREFERENCES

Teachers' preferences heavily influence scheduling decisions. Teachers' assessments of the classes they are currently teaching should partially determine their assignments for the following year. Assigning teachers contrary to their preferences can result in problems for everyone. Students' disruptive behaviors may increase, resulting in unpleasantness for students, teachers, principal, and parents.

Radical reassignments can disturb teachers. For example, teachers generally have strong feelings about the level of courses they teach, particularly if the courses involve the highest or lowest achieving students. If the master schedule requires a teacher to relinquish an honors class to teach a lower level course, the teacher and even the entire subject area team need to provide input. Or, a teacher who prefers remedial classes should have his say prior to being asked to teach advanced courses.

TRUST

A principal new to a building has not established trust; the process of assigning teachers to classes, therefore, is difficult. A teacher may perceive assignment of low level classes as a lack of faith in her instructional ability or even as an act of hostility. To avoid misunderstandings, the teaching team could make course assignments. For example, if six honors, fourteen average, and four low level math courses are needed at particular periods of the day, the math team decides who will teach each class. They consider which classes each taught the prior year as well as which levels they prefer to teach. The important point is that the math team make the decision.

SHARED DECISION MAKING

A principal who makes scheduling decisions in conjunction with the staff is more likely to be rewarded with quality judgments that have a high degree of staff acceptance and long-lasting results. Whenever possible, decisions regarding scheduling and assigning should utilize input from those directly affected.

Other

COURSES

What are the attitudes of teachers and parents toward the courses currently being offered? Are there enough electives, and do these meet the needs of students? Do the courses meet state requirements? Do parents of high achieving students want advanced courses that satisfy both high school and college requirements? Parents' and students' interest in soccer creates pressure on the school to include this sport in the athletic program. Such requests must be answered, and the principal must be prepared to justify the decisions.

Some courses, such as athletics, are better scheduled at particular times of the school day and depend on facilities available. Do coaches prefer to practice the first or last period of the day? Will boys' and girls' athletics be at separate times? During basketball season, will several grade levels as well as boys' and girls' teams need to share the gymnasium? Coaches are the best resource for resolving these issues.

Does each period offer enough classes to make room for each student? Electives account for a high number of student seats. Teacher complaints and student discipline problems increase when students have little interest in the electives. In a middle school where classrooms were crowded, adding a half-day art teacher may solve the seat-count problem, the student demand for design courses, and some special needs students' requests for drawing classes. The principal must not only make sure enough seats are available each period but also discover the students' interests and explore new course offerings. Student committees are one vehicle for such exploration.

Each state has its own standards for course listings. For core courses, titles and content usually must meet state accreditation requirements, while electives are less rigidly monitored. For example, when one school simply changed the title of a reading course for heterogeneously grouped students, the result was loss of state-provided textbooks. Staying abreast of state guidelines is crucial.

LUNCH PERIODS

How long are the lunch periods? How many shifts are needed to accommodate the student body? Who will supervise the cafeteria? Is the current practice creating problems for teachers or students? For example, the necessity of three lunch periods creates split classes. The class meets for 25 minutes, breaks for lunch, and returns for the final 25 minutes. Is this best for instruction? Sometimes teachers have lunch duty in lieu of teaching during the mid-day period. Is this the best use of teacher time, or should a hired community helper monitor lunch periods? If lunch periods are long, can students with extra time be released outdoors or to monitored study areas? Finding out where the problems are and ways to solve them begins by talking with cafeteria workers, teachers, and students. Schools often experiment with a variety of arrangements before finding one that solves the most problems.

DISTANCE LEARNING CLASSES

Some school districts, particularly those in rural areas, are increasingly turning to technology to fill gaps in their course offerings. For example, if the cost of hiring a teacher for advanced level math classes is prohibitive, or if specialists in distant cities can enhance the learning of science students, districts link with each other and with universities technologically to provide these advantages for their students. In some instances, secondary students are able to gain college credit as well for distance learning classes, although the students never leave their home campus.

Although rewarding to students, distance learning poses scheduling problems for principals. Courses offered from a distant site may begin and end at times that do not coincide with other schools' schedules, requiring flexible scheduling. Such adjustments are major if any of the schools are on nontraditional schedules such as block, accelerated, or modified block. Also, grading policies must be agreed upon and mechanisms in place for timely transfer of materials from one site to another.

A principal needs to ponder the considerations just described when planning the school schedule. The particular school determines the weight given to each. A school that is considering a change to teaming or block scheduling must face additional considerations.

ADDITIONAL CONSIDERATIONS

Some considerations merit attention for major changes such as teaming or some forms of block scheduling. First are listed those applicable to change in general, then those unique to block scheduling and teaming.

Change Issues

TEACHERS' LEVEL OF INVOLVEMENT, COMMITMENT, AND TRUST

Sergiovanni (1995) speaks of teachers who are "origins" and those who are "pawns." Pawns feel powerless and assume that forces outside their control determine what happens at school. Origins find work meaningful, purposeful, sensible, and significant; feel they have control over their work events; and take responsibility for themselves and what they do at work. Involvement for these teachers goes beyond the classroom because their commitment is to all aspects of the school. If an assessment of a teaching staff indicates that many of the teachers are origins, a climate for reform is likely to be present. If not, building trust, encouraging commitment, insisting on accountability, and increasing motivation should precede change. Sharing decisions with the staff enhances all of these goals.

SHARED DECISION MAKING

Wood, Nicholson, and Findley (1985) warn, "The weakness, if not failure, of many programs is often attributable to a program structure that has not attempted to involve the teacher emotionally or intellectually in the educational activity" (p. 142). Lunenburg and Ornstein (1996) discuss the benefits of sharing decisions. These are important when change is considered.

(1) The quality of the decision is increased when the knowledge and ideas of a group are combined.
(2) Participation by more than one person leads to more creative thinking, which often results in more feasible solutions.
(3) The decision is more likely to be accepted by the group if each person has been a part of the process.
(4) When group members have been involved in the decision-making process, understanding is increased.

(5) Groups can identify alternatives effectively because of the combined knowledge of the group.

(6) Major errors are more likely to be avoided as group members evaluate suggestions.

Staff involvement can take the form of visiting schools, researching the literature, and debating the advantages and disadvantages of various schedules. It can also include placing the master schedule in a place where the faculty can view its development and volunteer solutions to problems.

CENTRAL OFFICE SUPPORT

The superintendent and board probably approved the current schedule. Innovation requires full conceptual and financial backing from the superintendent, board, curriculum director, and others who have vested interest. For example, both block scheduling and teaming require considerable budgetary allowances for such components as additional staff, training, and resources, which the board must approve. Emotional support of the parents is central to school improvement. Central office staff can help garner that support by standing behind the school's decision.

COMMUNITY SUPPORT

The principal needs to know how the school's community perceives the school. Is there a history of conflict? Does it trust in the teachers and administrators? Communities are reluctant to support change unless they understand and approve the objectives and the consequences for their children. Talk of heterogeneous grouping for math is likely to alarm parents of high achieving students. The principal needs to include parents and the community throughout change, which may prolong the process but will greatly increase the probability of success.

SUPPORTING RESEARCH

Each school has years of experience to support whatever schedule is in place, and teachers can likely articulate the advantages they experience. When considering a major change, carefully research and assess the effectiveness of a specific reform before rushing headlong into its adoption. The research should clearly articulate expected benefits of the reform. For example, research to date is insufficient to support the notion that student achievement will increase when class time is increased; in fact, numerous reports indicate the contrary (Schroth & Dixon, 1996; Spencer & Lowe, 1994; Guskey & Kifer, 1995). Yet schools have adopted block scheduling, anticipating improved achievement scores.

Block Scheduling Issues

SPECIAL EDUCATION STUDENTS

Block scheduling requires students to spend longer periods of time with each teacher. Will regular teachers anticipate difficulties of special education students in classes of longer duration? Will teachers expect that special needs students are easier to handle in teaming situations where problems are shared by groups of teachers who have time to meet together with parents and to plan uniform strategies? A combination of block scheduling and teaming may be the best choice for teachers and students, because this allows teachers the flexibility of moving special students from one situation to another, depending on the activity.

PLANNING TIME

Block scheduling and teaming can significantly increase teachers' preparation time. Research shows that successful teaming requires one period for planning and one for team development (Merenbloom, 1991). An alternate day, block schedule usually includes 90-minute planning periods, which teachers are likely to appreciate. Yet some school boards and superintendents may determine that increased planning time is too expensive or unnecessary. Board and superintendent approval must precede such a change in teacher release time.

COURSES

Daily drill and practice for math, band, choir, and athletics will not occur when an alternate day, block scheduling model is adopted, because classes meet for 90 minutes every other day. Pressure from parents and teachers for daily meetings for some subjects may require adjustments. For example, some schools adopt a format where lower achieving students attend 90 minutes of math each day and every other day for other subjects (Schroth & Dixon, 1996). In states that limit athletic practice to 60 minutes a day, splitting a 90-minute block to include a 30-minute study hall satisfies all requirements.

Teaming Issues

ABILITY GROUPING

When a team of teachers shares a specific group of students, how will those pupils be grouped — by ability or heterogeneously? While some reformers advocate heterogeneous grouping, such a change is likely to bring an outcry from parents accustomed to differentiation based on ability. In a review of 27 studies on grouping, Slavin (1993) found that ability grouping had no effect on achievement. Yet, parent groups and some teachers demand differentiated levels for subjects such as math or reading. Leveling a group of 125–150 students, the size of many teams, requires careful planning; and giving teachers the flexibility to group and regroup the students throughout the day facilitates the process.

STUDENT PLACEMENT

All students must be placed with nonteam teachers two periods a day to provide the team's teachers common planning and teaming time. During these two periods, students must attend elective classes or pull-out programs, for example, band, gifted and talented class, athletics, Chapter I, or vocational programs. Thus, students are placed on a team according to student interests, talents, or particular needs. Athletics presents a problem for team selection, because coaches prefer to conduct these the first or last period of the day, requiring athletes to be placed together on one team. Because athletics usually involves a large number of students, a team could consist entirely of athletes.

SIZE OF SCHOOL

The size of the school influences scheduling choices. The student body may not be large enough to form teams or, in rural schools where teachers and students interact outside as well as in school, traditional scheduling may be adequate. On the other hand, if the school is large and impersonal, teaming can allow more opportunities for personal teacher–student contact.

Numerous scheduling considerations surround scheduling in general as well as specific change planning. Some of these have been addressed here. Discussions with staff in schools where change has been successful may clarify expectations. Confronting crucial decisions early in the change process increases the probability of successful implementation.

ADVANTAGES AND DISADVANTAGES OF VARIOUS SCHEDULING MODELS

The scope of scheduling considerations is far reaching, and seeking a viable solution is difficult. Adopting any particular scheduling model results in some losses as well as gains for the school. Descriptions of traditional, block, and teaming models as well as listings of likely advantages and disadvantages of each follow. Examine the pros and cons of each model when deciding which one best meets the school's needs.

Traditional Scheduling

Most common in American public schools still is the self-contained classroom for early grades and the Carnegie Unit of 50-minute class periods for older students.

SELF-CONTAINED CLASSROOMS

In self-contained classrooms typical of elementary schools, a single teacher is in charge of instructing twenty to thirty students for the major portion of the day, sending students out for a few subjects such as physical education, music, and art. The advantages of self-contained classrooms include

(1) For students
   - strong student–teacher relationships
   - firm student to student relationships
   - variety in grouping within the class
(2) For teachers
   - flexibility in time spent on subject areas
   - no need to undergo change if current arrangement is suitable and stable
   - buildings designed for self-contained classes

A major cost lies in the loss of high quality instruction for some subject areas, and possibly in all subjects if the teacher is not a master of instruction and discipline.

50-MINUTE CLASS PERIODS

The traditional 45- to 50-minute class period, shown in Figure 3.1, is of fixed length, and classes meet the same hour each day. The benefits include the following:

(1) For students
- Daily drill and practice is available for subjects such as math.
- Physical activity is afforded by frequent class changes.
- When absent, only one class period in each subject is missed.
- When transferring, schools are likely to be similar.

(2) For teachers
- Traditional scheduling is well known and requires no change.
- Itinerant teachers and specialists can be easily blended into the schedule.
- Buildings are designed for this arrangement.

Disadvantages may include the following:

(1) For students
- Periods are too short for extended teaching activities such as science labs and field trips.
- Teachers who know students personally are able to individualize instruction, but short class periods allow insufficient time for quality student–teacher relationships to form.
- Discipline problems can occur during the frequent passing periods, problems that tend to spill over into the classroom.

(2) For teachers
- 150 and more students are instructed each day.
- The class period, not instruction, determines activity length.

Block Scheduling

Block scheduling is one response to (a) the need to budget time more wisely and (b) teachers' desire for increased flexibility. Of the many configurations possible under the umbrella "block scheduling," the following appear most frequently in the literature. These all include longer class periods for at least part of the school day.

Period	Math 7th Jones	Math 8th Smith	Science 7th Joe	Science 8th Mims	English 7th Toms	English 8th Abott	Social studies 7th Sole	Social studies 8th Hughes	Reading Dunbar	Reading Tool	Electives Typing	Electives Art/Life Skills	Electives P.E./Athletics
1	Seat Count Course Number										1st Term/2nd Term	Art	Athletics Boys
2												Art	P.E.
3	Planning Period											Art	P.E.
4												Life Skills	P.E.
5							LUNCH					Life Skills	P.E.
6												Life Skills	P.E.
7												Life Skills	Athletics Girls

* All Periods are 45 minutes

Figure 3.1 Traditional seven-period day schedule for seventh and eighth grades.

ALTERNATE DAY, BLOCK SCHEDULE

Sometimes termed the A/B block schedule, this eight-period schedule allows for longer (90 or more minutes) classes but where half of the classes meet each day as shown in Figure 3.2. Four classes meet on A days, four on B days, with days of the week alternating as A or B. Teachers teach three classes and have a 90-minute conference period daily.

FLEXIBLE BLOCK SCHEDULE

For some schools, a combination of the traditional and alternate day, block schedule is most useful. For example, as shown in Figure 3.3, all eight classes meet on Monday, Wednesday, and Friday for 45 minutes each. The rest of the week's classes are 90 minutes long with even numbered class periods meeting one day a week and odd numbered the other day. Any combination of traditional and longer periods is possible. This allows for some longer instructional blocks for each subject each week.

	A Day	B Day	A Day	B Day	A Day
8:30-10:00	Period 1	Period 5	Period 1	Period 5	Period 1
10:10-11:40	Period 2	Period 6	Period 2	Period 6	Period 2
11:40-12:20	Lunch				
12:20-1:50	Period 3	Period 7	Period 3	Period 7	Period 3
2:00-3:30	Period 4	Period 8	Period 4	Period 8	Period 4

* All Periods are 90 minutes

Figure 3.2 Alternate (A/B) day block schedule.

Monday	Tuesday	Wednesday	Thursday	Friday
Periods	Periods	Periods	Periods	Periods
1	1	1	5	1
2		2		2
3	2	3	6	3
4		4		4
LUNCH				
5	3	5	7	5
6		6		6
7	4	7	8	7
8		8		8

* Monday, Wednesday, and Friday classes are 45 minutes in length; Tuesday and Thursday classes are 90 minutes in length.

Figure 3.3 Flexible block schedule.

FLUID BLOCK SCHEDULE

Shown in Figure 3.4, the 90-minute block and traditional periods can be combined within the school day with the fluid schedule. For example, students may be assigned to three 90-minute periods and two traditional 45-minute class periods. Here, also, any number of combinations is possible, depending on how many traditional periods are desired. For some schools, this allows for athletics, math, and foreign language classes to meet daily while giving subjects such as science longer periods for labs.

Some advantages of longer class periods may be as follows:

(1) For students
- The number of subjects students take in a year is increased.
- There is time for developing more meaningful teacher–student relationships.
- Daily homework is assigned for half as many classes.
- In-class conflicts are afforded a two-day cooling-off period.
- Passing periods are reduced, which may decrease discipline problems and increase class time when daily routines such as taking attendance occur less frequently.

(2) For teachers
- Planning periods are 90 minutes long.

- Instruction is delivered to fewer students daily.
- The number of papers to grade each day is reduced.
- Opportunities exist for creativity in classroom instruction and in-depth learning.
- A friendly, relaxed classroom climate is possible.
- Modular scheduling (planning in smaller units of time such as 15 or 20 minutes) is available, which allows for variety in activities and teaching methods.

Accompanying disadvantages to block scheduling merit consideration:

(1) For students
- When schedule gaps are filled with study halls, students may spend time in nonspecific study time with minimal supervision.
- The amount of time each class meets is reduced; for example, a 50-minute class that meets daily accrues 500 minutes of class time in two weeks; the same class meeting for 90 minutes every other day totals only 450 minutes in that same period of time (advocates of block scheduling argue that this time is more than made up for in the reduction in occurrence of daily routines such as taking attendance).

Times	Monday Periods	Tuesday Periods	Wednesday Periods	Thursday Periods	Friday Periods
8:00-9:30	1	6	1	6	1
9:35-11:05	2	7	2	7	2
11:10-11:55	3	3	3	3	3
12:00-12:30	LUNCH				
12:35-2:05	4	8	4	8	4
2:10-2:55	5	5	5	5	5

* Periods 3 and 5 are 45 minutes; all others are 90 minutes

Figure 3.4 Fluid block schedule.

- Some subjects require daily meetings (math, band, athletics).
(2) For teachers
    - New instructional methods are required.
    - Staff development and training sessions occur prior to and during implementation.
    - Extensive planning is needed, particularly the first year.
    - Curricula and textbooks are not adapted to longer class periods.
    - Substitutes may not be prepared for longer class periods.
(3) For the school
    - Additional materials and supplies will be needed for the increased number of subjects in which students enroll.
    - Staff, central office, parent, and community support must be available.
    - The budget may not support the increase in staff that will most likely be needed.

Some schools use other, less widely adopted forms of block scheduling.

SEMESTER BLOCK SCHEDULE

Sometimes termed the 4 × 4 block system or the intensified block schedule, this arrangement allows students to complete four classes each semester, attending each class for 90 minutes daily (see Figure 3.5). The benefits to teachers and students are much the same as for other forms of block scheduling with additional incentives:

(1) For students
    - Homework is easier to manage with fewer subjects.
    - Teacher to student and student to student relationships are intensified.
    - Efforts are concentrated without distractions.
    - A failed subject can be retaken the same year.
(2) For teachers
    - Opportunities for collaborative work are increased.
    - The mid-year slump is avoided.
    - Teachers teach fewer classes each semester.

A major difficulty, other than those listed earlier for block scheduling, is coordinating instruction for transfer students.

Times	Semester One 18 Weeks	Semester Two 18 Weeks
8:30-10:00	Course 1	Course 5
10:10-11:40	2	6
11:40-12:20	Lunch	
12:20-1:50	3	7
2:00-3:30	4	8

* All Periods are 90 minutes

Figure 3.5 Semester block schedule.

75-30-75 PLAN

Proposed by Canady and Rettig (1993), the school year is divided into three blocks of time, two 75-day terms and a 30-day term (see Figure 3.6). During each 75-day term, the school day includes three 112-minute block classes, one 48-minute period, 24 minutes for lunch, and 12 minutes for class changes. The 30-day term offers students the opportunity to study one core course intensively, or two electives, or retake a failed class. This plan can also take the form of 75-15-75-15 where two 15-day intersessions offer students the advantages of remediation or acceleration of their studies. Again, a drawback is coordination of studies for transfer students.

PARALLEL BLOCK SCHEDULING

Also proposed by Canady and Rettig (1992) and Canady and Fogliani (1989), this plan is designed for elementary as well as middle schools. An eight-period day is outlined but pull-out programs such as Chapter I, resource classes, talented and gifted, computer labs, and band are built into the instructional program so as to reduce class size for some classes, such as reading and math where small group work is desired. For example, while a small group of students remains with the teacher for reading, the rest of the class is scattered among the pull-out programs. Traditional scheduling offers similar advantages when classes

	Semester 1 75 Days	Semester 2 30 Days	Semester 3 75 Days
8:30- 10:15	Course 1	5	Course 6
10:20- 12:05	2		7
12:10- 12:40	Lunch	Lunch	Lunch
12:45- 1:30	3	3 Year-long Elective	3
1:35- 3:20	4	5	8

* Period 3 is 45 minutes; all others 105 minutes

Figure 3.6 *75-30-75 day plan.*

for lower achieving students are reduced by increasing class sizes in other classes.

TRIMESTERS

Rather than dividing the school year into two semesters of about 90 days each, the trimester plan allows for three separate semesters of about 60 days (see Figure 3.7). This plan is less widely used, poses problems for transfer students, and may not receive state accreditation when the number of hours students spend in class is below minimum requirements.

Teaming

For years, elementary school teachers have acknowledged the value of integrating instruction to blur the lines between subject areas and stress the links between fields of knowledge. A shift toward a more student-centered approach to the education of middle school students became more prevalent with the publication of *Turning Points* (Carnegie Council on Adolescent Development, 1989). An accompanying change has been the creation of interdisciplinary teams who provide continuity for group membership and instruction, similar to what exists at the elementary level. In fact, teaming—or schools within

Advantages and Disadvantages of Various Scheduling Models 59

schools—has probably become the definitive characteristic of the middle school concept (Mac Iver, 1990; Jenkins & Jenkins, 1991).

As with block scheduling, teaming can take on a variety of forms: most frequently cited are teaming, interdisciplinary teaming, and flexibly blocked teams (Merenbloom, 1991; Jacobs, 1989). For simple teaming, two or more teachers of two or more subjects share a common group of students (Figure 3.8). Students can be grouped and regrouped during the shared time period depending on the activity. Interdisciplinary teaming requires more complex configurations to coordinate instruction across disciplines to offer a less fragmented and more relevant curriculum. Thematic units are the usual planning tools for this type of integration. The flexibly blocked team, sometimes termed the team block schedule, not only incorporates the sharing of a common set of students and the opportunity for a coordinated curriculum but also the flexibility to determine the optimum use of the instructional time. Control and use of time are turned over to the teaching team. When students will attend electives is the only scheduling decision made by the principal. This format is similar to that of elementary schools where teachers are told when subjects such as physical education and music will occur but are free to flexibly schedule reading, math, social studies, and science on a daily basis.

Advantages are numerous to creating smaller units within the larger school setting as flexibility is increased.

	Trimester 1 60 days	Trimester 2 60 days	Trimester 3 60 days
8:30– 11:00	Course 1	Course 3	Course 5
11:10– 11:55	Year-long Course 7		
12:05– 12:35	Lunch	Lunch	Lunch
12:45– 3:15	2	4	6

* Course 7 is 45 minutes; all others are 2 1/2 hours

Figure 3.7 Sixty-day trimester block schedule.

Period	Team One	Team Two	Team Three
1	Teacher Planning/ Student Elective	Core Subject	Core Subject
2	Teacher Planning/ Student Elective	Core Subject	Core Subject
3	Core Subject	Teacher Planning/ Student Elective	Core Subject
4	Core Subject	LUNCH	Core Subject
5	LUNCH	Teacher Planning/ Student Elective	LUNCH
6	Core Subject	Core Subject	Core Subject or Tutoring
7	Core Subject	Core Subject	Teacher Planning/ Student Elective
8	Core Subject or Tutoring	Core Subject or Tutoring	Teacher Planning/ Student Elective

* All periods are 45 minutes

Figure 3.8 Teaming: grade six (seven-period day).

(1) For students
- Grouping and regrouping is possible, depending upon activity and subject matter.
- Teachers get to know and care for pupils personally as they interact with fewer students daily.
- Studies report improvement in thinking and learning skills as well as the ability to make connections between contexts that otherwise appear separate (Jacobs, 1989).
- Stable friendships can develop.
- Individualized instruction is attained more easily as teachers share tasks necessary to implement individual programs.

(2) For teachers
- Class time is flexible and determined by student learning needs.
- Various skills and strengths are utilized.
- Changes within the team do not interfere with other school teams' plans, for example, a scheduled field trip.
- Communication is increased, by necessity.

- The team collectively assumes responsibility for each student's learning and meets with parents as a group.

Grouping students and teachers by teams has drawbacks:

(1) For students
- Ability grouping may be more difficult to schedule.
- Interpersonal problems between teachers and between students are intensified due to increased time spent together.

(2) For teachers
- An adjustment period is required before the team operates smoothly, particularly with interdisciplinary instruction.
- Teachers must make a personal decision to join a team.
- Staff development is needed for integration of subject matter, for team building, and to learn conflict management techniques.

(3) For the administrator
- A common team planning time, core to teaming, as well as individual planning periods must be built into the schedule, requiring an increase in faculty members or the overloading of current classes.
- Team planning meetings require administrative monitoring.
- Budget adjustments are needed for curriculum development, increased staff, and additional materials necessary for changes in teaching methods.
- Support from central office, parents, and community must be obtained.
- Buildings are not designed for division of classrooms according to teams.

Whatever the scheduling choice, grouping or not grouping is an important matter. Because the issue is controversial, teacher, student, and parent involvement from the start will help reduce problems.

Selecting from the alternatives or creating a new scheduling model designed to meet the particular needs of the school is difficult. There is not one right schedule; the choice must finally be made on the basis of what most benefits students, not because a particular model is the current trend or because it provides more benefits to teachers or administrators. Hackmann (1995) lists ten guidelines for implementing new scheduling. One of these is to brainstorm creative alternatives. Says Hackmann, "Resist the temptation to simply adopt another school's model; it may be totally inappropriate for you. . . . Encourage teachers to 'think outside the box,' asking, 'What would we like to do that our current schedule does not allow?'. . . Remember, it's your program that drives the schedule, not the reverse" (pp. 25-26).

The next chapter directly addresses how to best implement scheduling for traditional, block scheduling, and teaming models and presents concrete step-by-step processes.

REFERENCES

Canady, R. L., & Fogliani. (1989, August). How to cut class size. *The Executive Educator*, *11*(8), 22-23.

Canady, R. L., & Rettig, M. D. (1992). Restructuring middle level schedules to promote equal access. *Schools in the Middle*, *1*(4), 20-26.

Canady, R. L., & Rettig, M. D. (1993, December). Unlocking the lockstep high school schedule. *Phi Delta Kappan*, *75*(4), 310-314.

Carnegie Council on Adolescent Development. (1989). *Turning points: Preparing American youth for the 21st century. The report of the task force on education of young adolescents*. Washington, DC: Carnegie Corporation.

Gusky, T. R., & Kifer, E. (1995, April). *Evaluation of a high school block schedule*. Paper presented at the Annual Meeting of the American Educational Research Association, San Francisco, CA.

Hackmann, D. G. (1995, November). Ten guidelines for implementing block scheduling. *Educational Leadership*, *53*(3), 24-27.

Jacobs, H. H. (1989). *Interdisciplinary curriculum: Design and implementation*. Alexandria, VA: Association for Supervision and Curriculum Development.

Jenkins, D. M., & Jenkins, K. D. (1991). The NMSA Delphi report: Roadmaps to the future. *Middle School Journal*, *22*(4), 27-36.

Lunenburg, F. C., & Ornstein, A. C. (1996). *Educational administration* (2nd ed.). Belmont, CA: Wadsworth Publishing Company.

Mac Iver, D. J. (1990). Meeting the needs of young adolescents: Advisory groups, interdisciplinary teaming teams, and school transition programs. *Phi Delta Kappan*, *71*, 458-464.

McPartland, J. M. (1989). *Balancing high quality subject-matter instruction with positive teacher-student relations in the middle grades* (Report No. OERI-G-86-0006). Washington, DC: Office of Educational Research and Improvement (ERIC Document Reproduction Service No. ED 291 704).

Merenbloom, E. Y. (1991). *The team process*. Columbus, OH: National Middle School Association.

Schroth, G., & Dixon, J. (1996, October). The effects of block scheduling on student performance. *International Journal of Educational Reform*, *5*(4), 472-476.

Sergiovanni, T. J. (1995). *The principalship: A reflective practice perspective* (3rd ed.). Boston: Allyn & Bacon.

Slavin, R. E. (1993, May). Ability grouping in the middle grades: Achievement effects and alternatives. *The Elementary School Journal*, *93*(5), 535-552.

Spencer, W. A., & Lowe, C. (1994, November). *The use of block periods for instruc-*

tion: A report and evaluation. Paper presented at the Annual Meeting of the Mid-South Educational Research Association, Nashville, TN.

Ubben, G. C., & Hughes, L. W. (1992). *The principal: Creative leadership for effective schools.* Boston: Allyn & Bacon.

Vroom, V. H., & Jago, A. G. (1988). *The new leadership: Managing participation in organizations.* Englewood Cliffs, NJ: Prentice-Hall.

Wood, C. L., Nicholson, E. W., & Findley, D. G. (1985). *The secondary school principal.* Boston: Allyn & Bacon.

CHAPTER 4

Constructing the Schedule

> *A deck of cards was built like the purest of hierarchies, with every card a master to those below it, a lackey to those above it. And there were "masses"—long suites—which always asserted themselves in the end, triumphing over the kings and aces.*
> —Ely Culbertson (1943)

Creating a master schedule is a process that occurs over an entire school year and involves, to various degrees, everyone from the school board to students. When successful, the master schedule represents superior use of staff and facilities for students' instructional benefit. This chapter provides step-by-step guidelines for constructing a traditional master schedule along with instructions for adapting this procedure to block scheduling formats and teaming. As some of the steps can be facilitated by technology, Appendix A lists computer programs available for scheduling purposes. Services, addresses, and phone numbers accompany a description of each program.

Hand scheduling is common in small schools, while larger schools generally rely on computer programs to expedite the process. Regardless of the method chosen, knowledge of the basic scheduling steps provides an understanding of what is required to create a master schedule. Even when relying on technology for major steps, knowing the underlying process allows the scheduler to make changes, solve problems, and hand schedule individual students if necessary.

CONSTRUCTING A MASTER SCHEDULE: TRADITIONAL MODELS

The master schedule can be judged by three criteria. First, to what

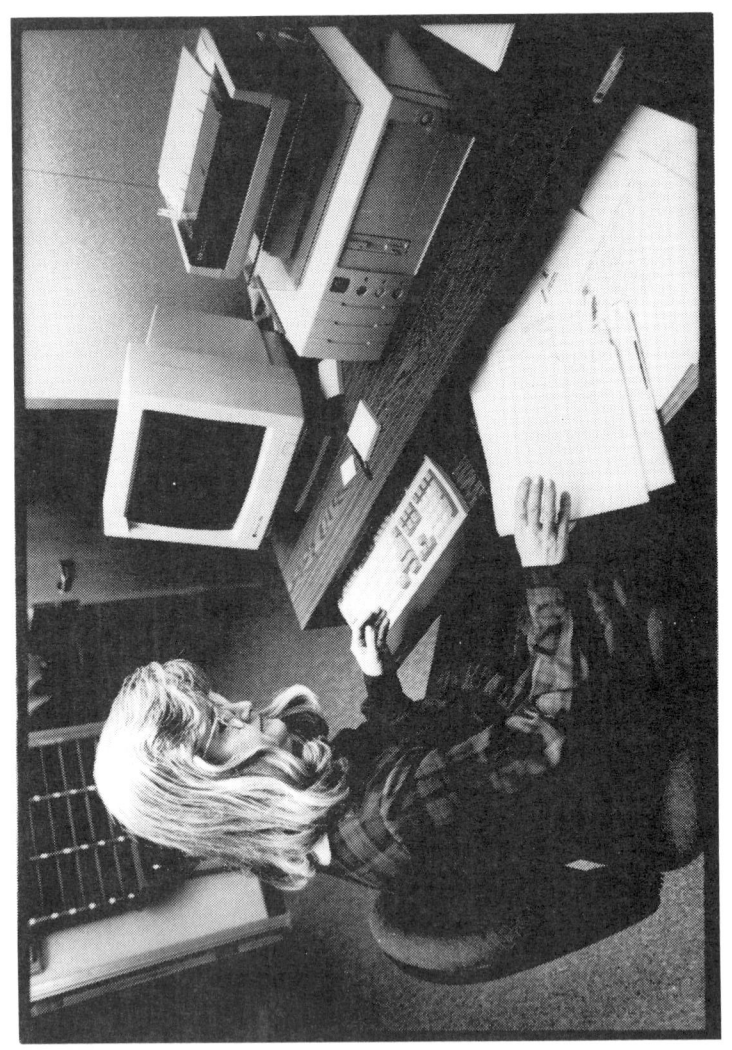

Computer programs can expedite scheduling.

degree does it accommodate student course requests? Second, is there an acceptable enrollment balance in multiple sections/classes of the courses scheduled? Third, to what extent have teachers' requests been satisfied? The following steps, basic to scheduling, outline a process that will help ensure meeting all three (Hanson, 1996).

Step One: Gather Information

The scheduler gathers the following information before constructing the master schedule:

- the number of teachers, their qualifications, and certifications
- courses for which teachers are competent and that they prefer to teach
- required courses for each grade level
- student preferences for electives
- a list of courses offered; superintendent and appropriate central office staff approval of these courses
- available classrooms and their capacity
- time and duration of classes
- type of schedule to be used (traditional, block, teaming)
- computer program for scheduling purposes
- teacher planning period needs
- special release periods, for example, athletic coaches
- special program needs (athletics, special education, band)
- how to advertise the curriculum and register students (in homeroom, large groups, and/or in parent meetings)

Step Two: Plan

Building next year's schedule begins during the first month of school when a scheduling plan is developed. Although the principal is ultimately responsible for the schedule, counselors and assistant principals often conduct many of the activities so they should be included in the planning phase. The plan encompasses the following:

(1) Specific activities that need to take place
(2) The time line for these activities
(3) Who should be responsible for their completion

The plan should look like this:

Activity	Person Responsible	Target Date
1. Review course offerings	Principal	September
2. Final approval of courses	Superintendent	November
3. Type of schedule selected/ computer software selection	Principal/ faculty	November/ December
4. Advertise curriculum/set registration procedures	Scheduler/ principal	December
5. Parent meetings	Principal	February
6. Student registration	Scheduler	February
7. Course tallies	Scheduler	February
8. Students edit and update course requests	Scheduler	March
9. Match courses with staff	Principal	March
10. List constraints (part-time teachers, off-campus programs) prepare materials for schedule construction	Principal/ scheduler/ secretaries	March
11. Construct master schedule	Principal/ scheduler/ teachers	April
12. Load student selections into computer (if used)	Scheduler	April
13. Adjust master schedule/resolve conflicts	Scheduler	May
14. Generate student, teacher, and room schedules; class lists; handout schedules to students	Scheduler	May/June

Step Three: Create Course Booklets

The course offerings booklet advertises the classes from which students make their selections. For each grade, the booklet contains a list of courses in which students are required to enroll and a list of available electives. Including a description of each course allows students to make informed choices. Differentiate semester courses from year-long courses with a notation for students to select either a year-long course or two semester courses for one elective period. For most efficient scheduling, number each course in the booklet according to a plan. Many schools number courses by department and grade level. For example, the first digit, 7, of English 7310 indicates this is a seventh grade course, the 3 shows it to be an English class, while the last two digits, 10, verify this is to be the tenth section of this particular English course. Some such plan is necessary for reading the schedule.

Step Four: Register Students

The course booklet is explained to students before registering for courses. For students entering the school, this activity is often conducted by counselors to ensure consistent presentation of information and academic counseling. Reviewing guidelines, answering questions, and actual registration can be conducted by counselors and teachers with large groups or smaller homeroom classes. In addition, parent meetings offer an opportunity to clarify questions and encourage parents' involvement in their children's decision making. Parent attendance can increase if some of the meetings are at night. For the grade level entering the school for the first time, meetings provide families the opportunity to tour the building and acquaint them with school guidelines and expectations. Providing information during registration reduces time spent later rescheduling students.

Electives are courses that students take in addition to the required courses. Students can prioritize three or four electives so, if the schedule cannot accommodate their first choice, a second or third choice can be substituted without having to contact the student. Some computer programs automatically make the substitutions from among several choices.

Step Four: Compute Course Tallies

Compile tallies for each course, by grade level. This permits the scheduler to know exactly how many seats, by grade level, to provide for every course. To obtain tallies, enter student requests for both semesters into the computer, or, in a small school, count these by hand. The partial list below indicates that 375 seventh graders have requested English 7310 and only ninety requested Art 7401.

Course Number	Course Title	Sex M/F	Student Requests	Grade 7	Grade 8
7310	Eng	175/200	375	375	0
7401	Art	60/30	90	90	0

Therefore, 375 English and ninety Art seats must be available sometime in the day. At this point, determine whether or not to drop a course due to insufficient interest or add a class.

Next, compute the number of sections for each course by dividing the number of student requests for a course by the number of students to be allowed in each class. In the example above, if a maximum of twenty-five students are to be allowed in each English class, fifteen sections will be needed to accommodate the 375 students. Thus, three teachers teaching seventh grade English five periods a day will suffice. If Art can accommodate thirty students each period, only three sections are necessary and taught by one half-day art teacher. The number of students allowed in each class determines the number of sections, and the number of sections indicates the number of teachers and their assignments.

The number of students allowed in each course varies considerably, depending on the subject, the number of teachers and aides assigned to a class, and the size of the classroom. For courses with high numbers of low achieving students, the teacher–student ratio should be fairly low. On the other hand, several coaches can teach seventy-five students one athletic period. A special education class for severely disabled students will likely have a teacher and several aides with ten or fewer students.

Step Five: Edit and Verify Selections

It is wise to correct registration errors and provide students an opportunity to make changes in their course requests. Teachers can help students verify their own course requests or alter their selections when provided a student request list. (A computer program can easily provide this list.) Corrections are then entered into the computer. Error-free data reduce time-consuming course changes once school begins in the fall.

Step Six: Generate a Conflict Matrix

The conflict matrix is an important document in master schedule construction. Minimizing course request conflicts, the matrix helps determine the course sections and their periods. The example of a partial matrix below shows that five students have enrolled in English 7310 as well as Art 7401. Therefore, five conflicts would occur if these were offered the same period. Twenty-four conflicts would arise if the English and Science classes coincided and seven if Art and Science occurred at the same time.

	English 7310	Art 7401	Science 7306
English 7310	0	5	24
Art 7401		0	7
Science 7306			0

Several sections of English and Science will accommodate the twenty-four students, but scheduling only one Art class and placing it during a period when English 7310 and Science 7306 are offered would eliminate conflicts.

Step Seven: Putting the Pieces Together

Some computer programs are able to calculate the step of assigning classes to specific periods of the day. Whether or not such a program is used, understanding this step is helpful when having to make adjustments later on in schedule construction.

MATERIALS

Place the master schedule on a large board in an accessible setting for teachers and administrators to view and manipulate. The large dry-erase, chalk, or foam boards ranging from 2 × 4 to 4 × 8 feet in size and marked off in a grid of rectangles about 1 × 2 inches are practical. The grid across denotes teachers, the other direction indicates periods of the day as shown previously in Figure 3.1. For each grade level, faculty are listed by department or by team. If a teacher crosses subject areas, he/she can be listed under each but care must be taken not to assign these teachers two courses in a given period.

Place rectangular paper (chips), color-coded for subject area and/or grade level with course number and maximum seats allowed, on the grid. They should be attached there so they can be moved around the board easily. The rectangles can be cut diagonally to differentiate single-semester from full-year courses. As shown in Figure 3.1 from the previous chapter, the scheduler(s) can rapidly scan the master schedule and experiment with a variety of course placements.

Schedule lunch by lengthening the mid-day period by the number of minutes alloted for lunch, no matter which type of scheduling model is used. Some teachers take their classes to lunch prior to holding class, others during the last portion of the period, and, if three lunch periods are necessary to accommodate all the students, others attend class, go to lunch, and return to finish the period.

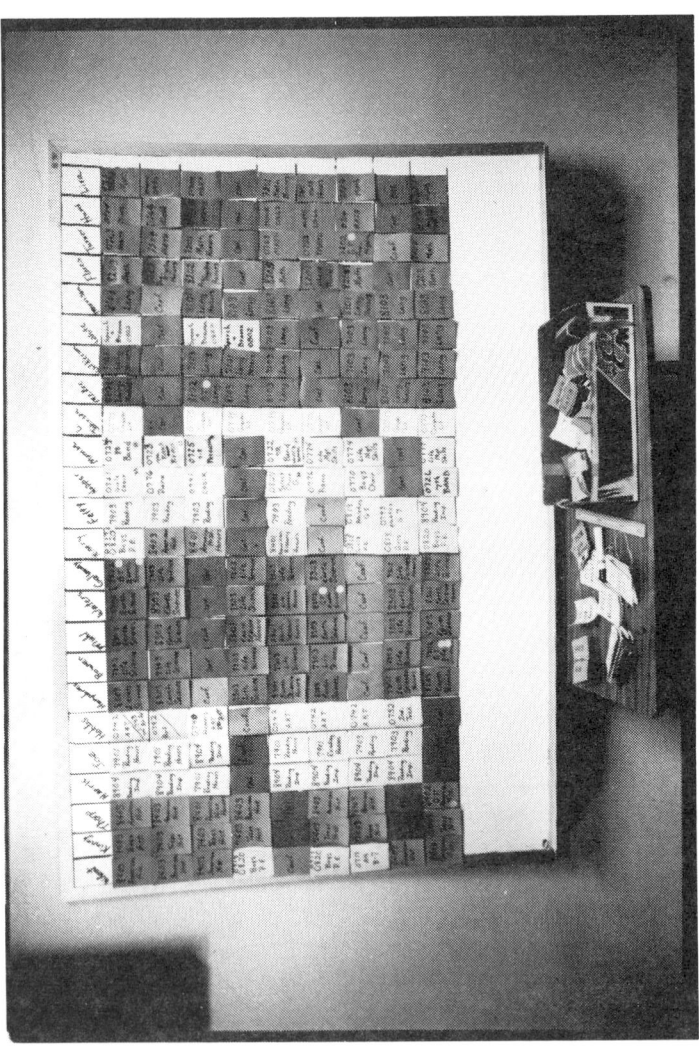

Sample of master schedule.

Once the student requests and factors that place constraints on the schedule such as classes offered in one particular period or a class with only one section are entered, some computer programs can create the master schedule.

PLACING COURSES: THOSE WITH CONSTRAINTS

First enter the courses that place the most constraints on the schedule. Follow the rest in descending order. Singletons are courses offered only once a day and doubletons twice. Examples of courses causing constraints are

- locked-in singletons (only offered during a specific period)
- locked-in multiple sections, such as band if offered two specific periods a day with an itinerant teacher
- sections assigned to part-time or shared-time teachers
- two or more sections that must be scheduled at the same time
- sections assigned to special rooms that are shared or have limited availability (an art teacher in the morning, a drafting teacher in the afternoon using the same room; or the gymnasium used by several grade levels)
- courses that have low enrollments and are combined to meet at the same time
- sections that require double or multiple period meetings, for example, vocational classes or teaming arrangements

Singletons with constraints are placed on the board first, followed by locked-in multiple sections with constraints. For example, if choir is offered one particular period (singleton) and beginning band two specific periods (a doubleton), choir is assigned first followed by band.

PLACING COURSES: THOSE WITHOUT CONSTRAINTS

After the courses with constraints are placed on the board, assign all courses that can meet any period in the schedule in this order:

- singletons (offered only once a day, for example, Seventh Grade Gifted and Talented or Girls' Choir)
- doubletons (classes requiring two sections, for example, when fifty students qualify for honors math, two sections will be needed; or when two sections of Girls' P.E. will be necessary to accommodate 100 or more seventh grade girls)

- tripletons (classes large enough to require three sections a day)
- quadrupletons (classes requiring four sections a day)
- five or more sections

RULES FOR BUILDING THE SCHEDULE: SINGLETONS

Some basic guidelines should be followed when placing singletons (classes that meet only one period a day such as Band or Girls' Choir) on the scheduling board.

(1) Place a singleton where is has no potential conflicts with any other singleton course that has already been scheduled in that period.
(2) If there already are other singleton courses scheduled into the period selected, use the conflict matrix to check potential conflicts.
(3) Continue to search for a placement that will conflict with the least number of other singletons. Sometimes rearranging the previously placed singletons is helpful.

RULES FOR BUILDING DOUBLETONS

Following some rules when placing doubletons facilitates schedule building.

(1) Compare the doubleton to every singleton in each period line when the teacher is available. Total the potential conflicts each period. For example, as shown in Figure 4.1, Mrs. Smith is to teach choir two of the six periods in the day but her planning time is first period, leaving periods two through six free for choir. Note also that periods five and six already have one singleton each and periods two, three, and four have two singletons.
(2) Place one leg of the doubleton in the period with the fewest potential conflicts; put the other leg in the period with the next fewest conflicts. In Mrs. Smith's case, schedule choir into periods five and six because these have the fewest conflicting singletons.
(3) Examine the board to verify if those two periods make sense and if the two legs are backed up against something that will lock students out. If so, move to the period with the third fewest conflicts.
(4) Place one leg (section) of the doubleton in the morning and the other in the afternoon, if reasonable. This accommodates more stu-

Constructing a Master Schedule: Traditional Models 75

	Jones	Kay	Bell	Toms	Adams	Stout	Total (Singletons)	Mrs. Smith
Period 1		Singleton			Singleton		2	Planning
2	Singleton		Singleton				2	Choir
3			Singleton			Singleton	2	
LUNCH								
4	Singleton			Siingleton			2	
5		Singleton					1	Choir
6					Singleton		1	

Figure 4.1 Placement of doubletons.

dents, as some classes are blocked over two or three periods and students are not available. So, in Mrs. Smith's case, choosing periods five and two may be best, even if period two has three singletons.

RULES FOR BUILDING TRIPLETONS

Following some specific rules for placing tripletons on the scheduling board also helps reduce conflicts.

(1) Count and record the seats available for each grade for each period. This is done by adding together the maximum number of students that can be placed into each class each period for a particular grade.

(2) Determine whether a teacher of one of the tripleton sections is available in the period with the fewest seats for the grade involved. If so, place one leg (section) in that period; if not, move to the period with the second fewest seats allocated. Follow the same pattern for the other legs of the tripleton. As shown in Figure 4.2, to strategically place three classes of Honors Math to benefit the most students, if the fewest seats are available periods two, four, and six (less than 275 seats each), and periods one, three, five, and seven have the most (275 or more), place the three Honors Math classes

Period	Math Sills 20	Science Joe 25	Science Lark 25	English Toms 20	English Mott 20	Social Studies Sole 25	Social Studies Gill 25	Reading Dunbar 20	Reading Zerbe 20	Typing 20	Electives Art/Life Skills 15/20	P.E./Athletics 60/50	Total Seats	Tripleton
1	Regular 7101	Regular 7201	Regular 7207	Regular 7301	Planning	Regular 7401	Modified 7407	Regular 7501	Modified 7507	7601	Art 15	P.E. 60	275	
2	Planning	Regular 7202	Regular 7208	Honors 7302	Regular 7307	Regular 7402	Planning	Honors 7502	Modified 7508	7602	Art 15	Athletics 50	240	Honors Math
3	Regular 7102	Regular 7203	Regular 7209	Regular 7303	Modified 7308	Honors 7403	Regular 7408	Regular 7503	Regular 7509	7603	Art 15	P.E. 60	295	
4	Modified 7103	Planning	Planning	Regular 7304	Regular 7309	Regular 7404	Regular 7409	Regular 7504	Regular 7510	7604	Life Skills 20	Planning	190	Honors Math
5	Regular 7104	Regular 7204	Regular 7210	Honors 7305	Regular 7310	Regular 7405	Modified 7410	Regular 7505	Planning	7605	Life Skills 20	P.E. 60	280	
6	Regular 7105	Regular 7205	Regular 7211	Planning	Modified 7311	Planning	Regular 7411	Regular 7506	Honors 7511	Planning	Life Skills 20	P.E. 60	235	Honors Math
7	Regular 7106	Honors 7206	Regular 7212	Regular 7306	Regular 7312	Honors 7406	Regular 7412	Planning	Modified 7512	7606	Life Skills 20	P.E. 60	280	

Figure 4.2 Seventh grade seat counts for placement of tripletons.

(tripletons) in periods two, four, and six (the fewest seats) if the teachers are available those periods.

(3) Confirm that the three legs of the tripleton are in three different periods of the day. If more than one teacher is involved in teaching the tripleton, the sections should be staggered so that two teachers do not teach two legs of the tripleton at the same time. Spreading the classes throughout the day offers more possibilities for matching student requests with the master schedule.

The grid should now be completely filled. Any gaps can be filled at a later date, as some classes may become overloaded when conflicts occur. The gaps allow room for manipulation of the schedule.

Step Eight: Count Seats

After all courses are assigned to a spot on the grid, obtain a seat count for each period for each grade so that any one period does not have an overabundance or far too few seats. Working across the board, by period and grade level, add together the maximum number of seats allowed for each class. This sum indicates whether enough places are available to place every student somewhere each period of the day. For example, if during first period, eight grade math classes can hold fifty students, science sixty, social studies forty, English fifty, and all electives together seventy, the total number of seats available to eighth graders is 270. If there are 300 eighth grade students, that period must have more seats available. Several options are possible. The number of seats allowed for each class can be increased; say, if English classes were held at twenty-five, increasing to thirty will provide for more students. Another possibility is to move classes, such as physical education, that usually hold large numbers of students, into that period. If physical education has created an inordinately high seat count another period, moving that class can solve problems for two periods. Having a few more seats available each period than students to be scheduled is important for flexibility.

Once balanced, enter the master schedule into the computer. That is, courses offered each period, teacher assignments, maximum number of seats for each course, and all constraints are officially placed in the computer, ready now to match with student requests. If a computer program is not used, the master schedule board is complete and ready for assigning students to classes.

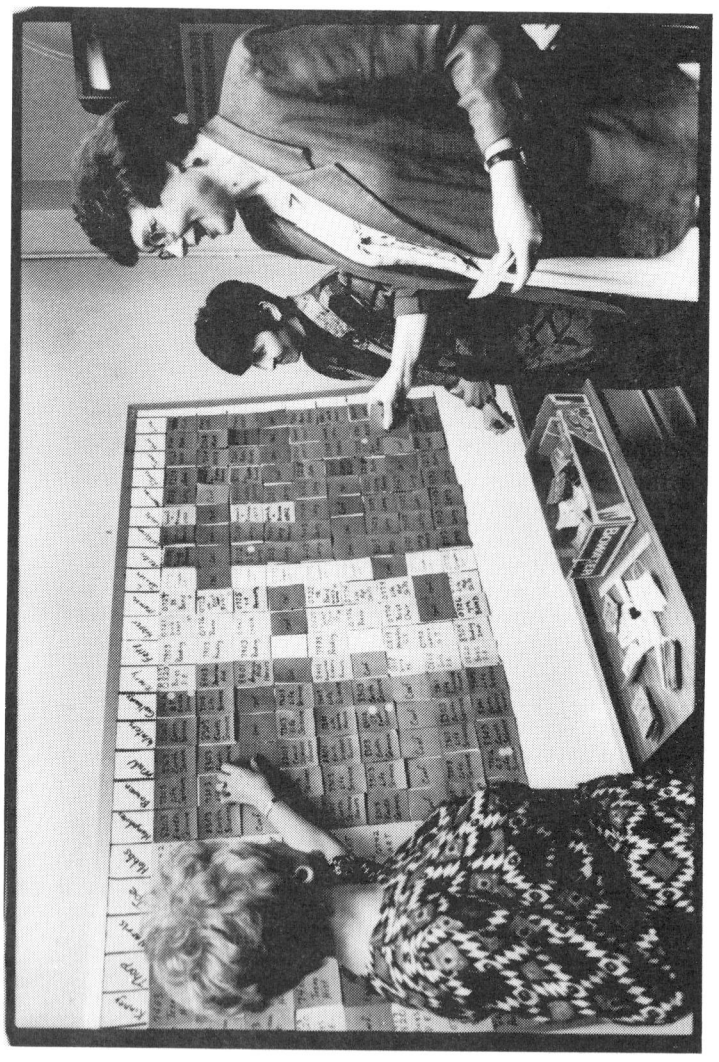
Teachers discuss schedule.

Step Nine: Match Students to Master Schedule

With the students' requests and the master schedule both in the computer, make a first run of the schedule to determine the number of students whose requests can be fully satisfied. If the first seven steps have been carefully followed, the number of student requests satisfied should be fairly high, and the computer can generate student schedules. If not, the next steps should increase the likelihood of a higher percentage of student requests being satisfied on the next run. If a computer program is not used, each student's requests are marked on the grid itself using an erasable hash mark. After all requests have been marked, totals are computed for each class.

Step Ten: Lock in the Schedule

After making course adjustments to satisfy as many student needs as possible, the schedule is considered complete and, for some computer programs, requires "locking in" the schedule. This means that shifting courses and changing student schedules must now be done manually, making it important that few, if any, further changes are made to the master schedule. If student requests are tallied by hand rather than with the use of a computer program, the schedule is now complete and should not be changed. Now print student schedules, and make them available for distribution. Figure 4.3 shows a partial computer printout of one school's final schedule, which indicates the section, lunch assignment, room, teacher, gender restrictions, and maximum number of students allowed for each semester.

Step Eleven: Generate Reports and Distribute Schedules

A number of reports are created for the convenience of the students and staff. Student schedules are generated so that students know before school begins which classes to attend which periods. Figure 4.4 shows a sample student schedule. Teachers need room assignments and class rosters. Copies of the master schedule should be available to school staff, secretaries, counselors, superintendent, and appropriate central office staff.

How and when students are to receive their schedules requires a plan, as parents and students often begin requesting these early in summer. Placing notices in local newspapers and radio announcements advertise

```
DATE 02/10/97                                                                                              PAGE      2
PRINT ONLY (SECTION)
COUNTY-116  DISTRICT-905                                                                     CAMPUS-041  LOCATION-872

                        SEM SEX REQ FRG TIE  C-M  PR-CTL VAL SCAN R/C GM-LBL GP-LVL CREDIT S/H DEP GRADE-AVAILIBILITY  TEA #  CODE P/S
0716  GIRL'S P.E.        4   G                      02    Y   Y    Y    Y      1    00.00   R      07                  03823000

                            SECT  LUN  MMP  ROOM  INST-NUMBER & NAME    SEX  MAX   SEM1  SEM2  SEM3   SEMESTER-PERIOD-PERIOD-DAYMET
                             01         1   GYM   059  HURD          F   G    25    20    21     0    4-02-02-0
                             02    A    1   GYM   059  HURD          F   G    25    18    19     0    4-03-03-0
                             03         1   GYM   059  HURD          F   G    25    18    18     0    4-06-06-0
                             04    A    1   GYM   059  HURD          F   G    25    19    20     0    4-07-07-0
                             05         1   GYM   056  MOMON         A   G    15     1     1     0    4-04-04-0

                        SEM SEX REQ FRG TIE  C-M  PR-CTL VAL SCAN R/C GM-LBL GP-LVL CREDIT S/H DEP GRADE-AVAILIBILITY  TEA #  CODE P/S
0717  BOY'S P.E.         4   B                      02    Y   Y    Y    Y      1    00.00   R      07                  03823000

                            SECT  LUN  MMP  ROOM  INST-NUMBER & NAME    SEX  MAX   SEM1  SEM2  SEM3   SEMESTER-PERIOD-PERIOD-DAYMET
                             01         1   GYM   012  TURNER        E   B    25    20    19     0    4-02-02-0
                             02    A    1   GYM   012  TURNER        E   B    25    15    15     0    4-03-03-0
                             03         1   GYM   012  TURNER        E   B    25    14    14     0    4-06-06-0
                             04    A    1   GYM   012  TURNER        E   B    25    17    18     0    4-07-07-0
                             05         1   GYM   005  TENERY        S   B    15    20    19     0    4-05-05-0

                        SEM SEX REQ FRG TIE  C-M  PR-CTL VAL SCAN R/C GM-LBL GP-LVL CREDIT S/H DEP GRADE-AVAILIBILITY  TEA #  CODE P/S
0718  ATHLETICS B7       4   B               YES    02    Y   Y    Y    Y      1    00.00   R  Z@  07                  03823000

                            SECT  LUN  MMP  ROOM  INST-NUMBER & NAME    SEX  MAX   SEM1  SEM2  SEM3   SEMESTER-PERIOD-PERIOD-DAYMET
                             01         1   FH    012  TURNER        E   B    25    18    18     0    4-05-05-0
                             02         1   FH    016  WHEAT         J   B    25    21    20     0    4-05-05-0
                             03         1   FH    058  KINNEY        R   B    25    19    19     0    4-05-05-0
                             04         1   FH    009  MUHL          K   B    25    16    16     0    4-05-05-0

                        SEM SEX REQ FRG TIE  C-M  PR-CTL VAL SCAN R/C GM-LBL GP-LVL CREDIT S/H DEP GRADE-AVAILIBILITY  TEA #  CODE P/S
0721  7TH GIRLS CHOIR    4   G               YES    02    Y   Y    Y    Y      1    00.00      Z@  07                  03154300

                            SECT  LUN  MMP  ROOM  INST-NUMBER & NAME    SEX  MAX   SEM1  SEM2  SEM3   SEMESTER-PERIOD-PERIOD-DAYMET
                             01         1   CR    035  MORRISON      M   G    50    23    23     0    4-01-01-0

                        SEM SEX REQ FRG TIE  C-M  PR-CTL VAL SCAN R/C GM-LBL GP-LVL CREDIT S/H DEP GRADE-AVAILIBILITY  TEA #  CODE P/S
0722  WOODWINDS          4                   YES    02    Y   Y    Y    Y      1    00.00      Z@  07,08               03154100

                            SECT  LUN  MMP  ROOM  INST-NUMBER & NAME    SEX  MAX   SEM1  SEM2  SEM3   SEMESTER-PERIOD-PERIOD-DAYMET
                             01         1   BH    057  LIRA          R        50    25    24     0    4-06-06-0

                        SEM SEX REQ FRG TIE  C-M  PR-CTL VAL SCAN R/C GM-LBL GP-LVL CREDIT S/H DEP GRADE-AVAILIBILITY  TEA #  CODE P/S
0723  BRASS              4                   YES    02    Y   Y    Y    Y      1    00.00      Z@  07                  03154100

                            SECT  LUN  MMP  ROOM  INST-NUMBER & NAME    SEX  MAX   SEM1  SEM2  SEM3   SEMESTER-PERIOD-PERIOD-DAYMET
                             01         1   BH    057  LIRA          R        50    11    12     0    4-04-04-0
```

Figure 4.3 *Master section data listing for 1996–97 school year.*

```
SM42      LOC 872                                                    02/10/97
116905    CHANGE        STUDENT SCHEDULE (CURR YR)                   11:15:28
        ------>STUDENT NAME<------
ID-NUM   LAST           FIRST         I  GEN SEX  --->ETH<---   GR RET  -ADVISOR-  WITHDRAW
004280   SMITH          STEVEN        K   B       5 WHITE       07      C-YR N-YR  DATE
ASSIGN ORIGINAL N
------------>SEMESTER 1<------------              ------------>SEMESTER 2<------------   CLASS OVERLOAD
A  PR CRS-SEC <--TITLE-->  ROOM INST            A  PR CRS-SEC <--TITLE-->  ROOM INST
   01 7301 03 LIFE SCI 7    101 HUMPHRI            01 7301 03 LIFE SCI 7    101 HUMPHRI
   02 0717 01 BOY'S P.E.    GYM TURNER             02 0717 01 BOY'S P.E.    GYM TURNER
   03 7202 02 GT PRE-ALG    219 LEWIS              03 7202 02 GT PRE-ALG    219 LEWIS
   04 7401 01 TX HIS HONO   208 HONZELL            04 7401 01 TX HIS HONO   208 HONZELL
   05 7901 02 READ 7 HONO   211 OGDEN              05 7901 02 READ 7 HONO   211 OGDEN
   06 7101 02 LANG 7 HONO   204 CASPER             06 7101 02 LANG 7 HONO   204 CASPER
   07 7202 02 GT PRE-ALG    219 LEWIS              07 7202 02 GT PRE-ALG    219 LEWIS
   08 0856 05 PHOTOGRAPHY   106 KING               08 0744 11 KEYBOARDING   109 WILKERS
```

"ENTER" = UPDATE   PF3 = MENU

Figure 4.4 Sample student schedule.

the date, time, and place of schedule distribution. A formal meeting for administrators to meet parents and students to receive their schedules is popular. After the meeting, student council members, cheerleaders, and athletes can be available to take new students on school tours, adding a personal touch.

BLOCK SCHEDULING MODELS

Building the master schedule for block scheduling generally requires following the eleven steps listed above for traditional scheduling. Deviation from the steps depends on the type of block scheduling implemented. The alternative forms of block scheduling will now be addressed in turn with suggestions for changes or additions to the above steps. As with traditional scheduling, computer programs vary in the degree to which they aid the scheduler in creating the master schedule. Most eliminate the laborious task of building the schedule outlined in step six, and some are even written specifically for block models.

Alternate Day, Block Scheduling

The alternate day, or A/B, block schedule allows for longer, usually 90-minute, class periods where half of the classes meet one day, the other half the next day (Figure 3.2 from Chapter 3). Periods one through four meet on A days; periods five through eight on B days. Teachers teach three classes and have a 90-minute conference period daily. Building the master schedule requires treating two days as one and following the eleven steps outlined for traditional scheduling. The master schedule board is simply divided in half so that periods one through four are clearly separated from periods five through eight, as shown in Figure 4.5. The format is identical to that of the traditional model shown in Figure 3.1 in Chapter 3 with the word "Lunch" replaced by "B Days" and an eighth period added at the end of the day. Thus the lower portion of the diagram. Periods five through eight are designated as alternating with periods one through four at the top. Students need to be notified to attend classes accordingly.

The split in the school day does present some obstacles. Some subjects, such as math, probably require daily meetings. Double blocking students into math, for example, allows them to attend 90 minutes of math daily and is fairly simple unless students are placed with the same

A Days

Time	Period	Dobbs	Smith	Toms	Zerbe	Schweers
8:30-10:00	1					
10:10-11:40	2					
11:40-12:20	Lunch					
12:20-1:50	3					
2:00-3:30	4					

B Days

Time	Period	Dobbs	Smith	Toms	Zerbe	Schweers
8:30-10:00	5					
10:10-11:40	6					
11:40-12:20	Lunch					
12:20-1:50	7					
2:00-3:30	8					

Figure 4.5 Constructing the master schedule: alternate day A/B block schedule.

teacher for both periods. In this case, link these courses when entering them into the computer. Precisely how they are linked depends upon the computer program used. With an alternate day schedule, school alternately begins with periods one and five, and ends with periods four and eight. Coaches frequently prefer athletics the first or last period of the day to extend practice time. Schools offering athletics to two grade levels for both boys and girls often place seventh grade boys in athletics first period and eighth grade boys fifth period. The boys then practice after school on the days they do not have class. This plan is reversed for the girls. Seventh grade girls' athletics is assigned to fourth period and eighth grade girls to eighth period at the end of the day with additional practice time scheduled before or after school on the days athletics is not conducted during the school day. Figure 4.6 shows one school's math teacher's schedule where classes are 90 minutes in length and A and B days are designated as Red and White Days. Included for each teacher in the first column is the room number, teacher identification number, and total number of students taught. The subsequent columns show the level of the course each period (Gifted, Honors, or Regular); the course number followed by the section (for example, 7201-01); and the total number of students in the class, written in by hand to facilitate changes throughout the year.

Another problem arises when itinerant teachers are bound by schedules of other schools to which they travel. These teachers may not have the flexibility to provide their services on alternate days for 90 minutes. Such issues must be resolved with other schools involved.

Chapter 3 discussed the advantages and disadvantages of all forms of block scheduling to students, teachers, and the school. As far as creating the master schedule is concerned, the format remains similar to traditional scheduling. Some computer programs are designed to specifically handle alternate day, block scheduling, eliminating the tedious task of building the schedule as outlined in step seven.

Flexible Scheduling

Some schools alternate traditional six- or eight-period days with the block scheduled days. Figure 3.3 from Chapter 3 is an example. Any number of variations of this model is possible. The six- or eight-period day can be interspersed with blocked days once, twice, or even three times a week. Follow the eleven steps outlined above when creating the master and student schedules. Two blocked days, together, are treated as one eight-period day. Problems created by this model are similar to those of alternate day scheduling. Some classes require daily drill and practice, athletics offered during the school day pose problems, and itinerant teachers' schedules may not mesh with the flexible schedule. Again, some computer programs adjust for flexible scheduling, greatly simplifying the entire process.

TEACHER	RED DAY 1ST PERIOD 7:45-9:20	RED DAY 2ND PERIOD ANNOUNCEMENTS 9:25-11:05	L U N C H	RED DAY 3RD PERIOD & LUNCH 11:10-1:10	RED DAY 4TH PERIOD 1:15-2:45	WHITE DAY 5TH PERIOD 7:45-9:20	WHITE DAY 6TH PERIOD & ANNOUNCEMENTS 9:25-11:05	L U N C H	WHITE DAY 7TH PERIOD & LUNCH 11:10-1:10	WHITE DAY 8TH PERIOD 1:15-2:45
RM 120 KEITH GRANT T= 118	HONORS MATH 23 7201-01	CONFERENCE	A	REGULAR MATH 15 7203-01	REGULAR MATH 21 7203-02	CONFERENCE	HONORS MATH 23 7201-01	A	REGULAR MATH 15 7203-02	REGULAR MATH 21 7203-02
RM 112 MIKE HALL T= 112	GT/HONORS PRE-ALGEBRA 11 7202-01	CONFERENCE	A	REGULAR MATH 19 7203-03	REGULAR MATH 24 7203-04	GT/HONORS PRE-ALGEBRA 11 7202-01	CONFERENCE	A	REGULAR MATH 19 7203-03	REGULAR MATH 26 7203-04
RM 216 RAY MOOD T= 150	REGULAR MATH 22 7203-05	CONFERENCE	B	HONORS MATH 28 7201-02	REGULAR MATH 25 7203-07	REGULAR MATH 22 7203-05	CONFERENCE	B	HONORS MATH 28 7201-02	REGULAR MATH 25 7203-07
RM 114 LIS TAYLOR T= 124	REGULAR MATH 26 7203-08	CONFERENCE	A	REGULAR MATH 21 7203-09	HONORS MATH 21 7201-03	REGULAR MATH 26 7203-08	CONFERENCE	A	REGULAR MATH 21 7203-09	HONORS MATH 21 7201-03
RM 217 EVE PERON T= 148	REGULAR MATH 23 8203-01	CONFERENCE	B	GT/HONORS ALGEBRA 29 8201-01	GT/HONORS ALGEBRA 32 8201-02	GT/HONORS ALGEBRA 32 8201-02	REGULAR MATH 23 8203-01	B	GT/HONORS ALGEBRA 29 8201-01	CONFERENCE
RM 116 SARA O'HARE T= 130	HONORS PRE-ALGEBRA 23 8202-03	CONFERENCE	A	REGULAR MATH 24 8203-02	REGULAR MATH 18 8203-03	HONORS PRE-ALGEBRA 23 8202-03	CONFERENCE	A	REGULAR MATH 24 8203-02	REGULAR MATH 18 8203-03
RM 218 RAY BUTLER T= 134	REGULAR MATH 22 8203-04	CONFERENCE	B	REGULAR MATH 23 8203-05	REGULAR MATH 22 8203-06	REGULAR MATH 22 8203-04	CONFERENCE	B	REGULAR MATH 23 8203-05	REGULAR MATH 22 8203-06
RM 105 PAT TIRE T= 122	REGULAR MATH 19 8203-07	CONFERENCE	C	REGULAR MATH 21 8203-08	REGULAR MATH 23 8203-09	REGULAR MATH 19 8203-07	CONFERENCE	C	REGULAR MATH 21 8203-08	REGULAR MATH 23 8203-09
RM 209 JOY CLOUD T= 146	REGULAR MATH 20 8203-10	CONFERENCE	C	HONORS PRE-ALGEBRA 28 8202-02	REGULAR MATH 25 8203-11	REGULAR MATH 20 8203-10	HONORS PRE-ALGEBRA 28 8202-02	C	CONFERENCE	REGULAR MATH 25 8203-11
RM 221 BOB JOY T= 133	REGULAR MATH 24 7203-10	CONFERENCE	B	REGULAR MATH 21 7203-06	REGULAR MATH 24 7203-11	REGULAR MATH 24 7203-10	CONFERENCE	B	REGULAR MATH 21 7203-06	REGULAR MATH 24 7203-11
RM 219 KATE WAYNE T= 142	REGULAR MATH 24 7203-12	CONFERENCE	B	GT/HONORS PRE-ALGEBRA 22 7202-02	HONORS PRE-ALGEBRA 25 8202-01	REGULAR MATH 24 7203-12	CONFERENCE	B	GT/HONORS PRE-ALGEBRA 22 7202-02	HONORS PRE-ALGEBRA 25 8202-01

Figure 4.6 Math teacher's schedule.

Fluid Block Schedule

The 90-minute blocked classes can be combined with traditional 45-minute periods within each school day as shown in Figure 3.4 from Chapter 3. Periods three and five are 45 minutes, and the rest are 90 minutes. With this blended design, some classes, such as band and athletics, can meet on a daily basis during periods three and five, while longer class periods are provided for other subjects. Many combinations are possible, depending on the number of traditional 45-minute periods desired. For some middle schools, a 30-minute period for teachers to advise or tutor students is built into this type of model.

Steps one through eleven outlined earlier for traditional scheduling are appropriate for fluid block scheduling as all classes meet at least once within the period of two days. While the scheduling board can show a master schedule similar to that of a traditional day, it is in the construction of a daily schedule for staff and students that the differences appear. Also, while some classes do not meet daily, teachers and students need to be clear about which classes to attend each day. While the problem of classes requiring daily drill and practice is solved with this model, receiving itinerant teachers' services is not.

Semester Block Schedule

This intensified course schedule allows students to complete four classes each semester, making a total of eight for the year (see Chapter 3, Figure 3.5). Students attend the same four classes for 90 minutes each day. Again, the eleven step process previously described is appropriate, but student schedules are outlined for a year rather than a semester. The scheduling board is divided in half, much as the alternate day schedule, so that one half denotes the first four periods (first semester) and the second half periods five through eight (semester two). As with an alternate day plan, lunch is scheduled after second period.

The same problems occur here as with the alternate day schedule. Daily drill and practice for some classes, boys' and girls' athletics, which are preferred first or last period, and blending the itinerant teachers' schedules all require special attention. It may be that combining the semester schedule with a traditional model where some classes meet daily for 45 minutes may eliminate some of these difficulties.

Other Models

The 75-30-75 plan divides the school year into three blocks of time: two 75-day terms and one 30-day intersession (see Chapter 3, Figure 3.6). The 75-day terms have schedules much as the fluid block schedule, which divides the school day between traditional and blocked periods of time. The separately scheduled, 30-day intersession offers either remedial or enrichment courses, and students take only one or two courses. Again, the eleven step process is appropriate but must be done separately for the 30-day session.

Parallel block scheduling calls for some classes to be reduced in size for subjects such as math and reading. To create the master schedule for this plan, follow the eleven step process but keep the seat count for math and reading between ten and fifteen for some periods of the day. Other courses offered during those same periods absorb the rest of the students.

The trimester plan breaks the school year into three semesters of about 60 days each as shown in Figure 3.7 from Chapter 3. Either traditional or block scheduling is suitable. Either way, the eleven step process is appropriate for placing students into classes and creating the master schedule. If a blocked plan is used, student schedules should be written for a full year. Some computer programs are designed to handle any of the less traditional models, thus simplifying the scheduling process.

THE TEAMING MODEL

Scheduling teams of teachers to be responsible for a core group of about 125 students for most of the day can be done in several ways. The method depends partially on the number of teams and teachers, how to select students for teams, and the choice of electives. See Figure 3.8 from Chapter 3 for an example of a team schedule.

It is assumed here that teachers have one period each day for team planning and one for personal planning. During team time, teachers plan interdisciplinary units of study, solve problems, and conference as a group with parents. For the remainder of the day, the students are assigned to English, reading, math, social studies, and science, a task that can be left to teachers to schedule flexibly according to instructional needs. A traditional model where students are scheduled into particular classes each period for 45 or 50 minutes is also popular.

Two arrangements simplify scheduling teams. The first is conducting athletics before or after school rather than during the school day, because all students on all academic teams must attend elective courses during the same two periods when teachers are planning. A problem occurs when athletics, an elective, is scheduled during the school day. This large group of athletes must be assigned to the team of teachers whose planning time is at the same time as the athletic period. If 125 boys are in athletics one period and so are assigned to a particular team, that team will have 125 males and about ten females, defeating the concept of heterogeneous grouping.

Second, assigning all students in a given grade to a few specific electives also reduces conflict. For example, if sixth grade students all take Spanish and physical education, half of the team attend Spanish during the first elective period and physical education during the second. The plan is reversed for the other half of the team. Thus, if the school has three sixth grade teams, the Spanish and physical education teachers are involved with that grade level six periods a day. When more electives are available and students from various levels are allowed in those courses, scheduling becomes increasingly complicated.

The composition of the teaching teams also affects scheduling. For some schools, teaming for two or three subject areas is considered adequate. For example, a team may consist of a math, a science, and a social studies teacher. The rest of the day, the students attend classes with students from other teams.

Selection of team members requires skillful planning. Conflicts between teachers on a team are not unusual, so careful placement and training in conflict resolution can help offset problems. Knowing the potential for friction, a principal may make the teaching assignments and then train teams in techniques designed to aid them in solving differences that may arise.

Placement of students on teams also requires planning. According to Merenbloom (1991), teachers need to be involved in designing and confirming the composition of teams, and pupils of various ability levels should be properly distributed among teams. Dispersing students evenly by sex and race is another issue for consideration.

While heterogeneous grouping of most students is advocated by middle school proponents, distributing small groups such as gifted or those with disabilities among all teams may not be reasonable. All gifted students may be placed on one team so the students can be taught through pull-out programs or by specially trained teachers placed on that team. Assigning students with severe disabilities to one team allows special education support staff to spend their time efficiently in one area where their help is most needed.

In order to maintain a "school within a school" atmosphere, teams need to be in separate parts of the building. As teams may be flexible in the use of their time, operating without bells can be less disruptive for everyone.

Creation of the master schedule can take several forms. First, students can be assigned to teams according to some plan by the principal or by teachers. For example, students can be sorted by ability level, sex, race, and special classifications so that all teams are balanced in regard to these characteristics. Thus, the team becomes a "school within a school" and is treated as such. A master schedule is then created for each team (see Chapter 3, Figure 3.8), similar to a traditional schedule. It designates periods as teacher conferencing and teaming times, and lists student electives for that team during those two periods. These constraints and student requests are entered into the computer, and student schedules are created.

A second method for scheduling teams is to allow the computer to sort out teams according to electives by using the traditional scheduling model. Thus, all the students who share electives two particular periods compose a team. Those whose electives fall into two other periods form another team, and so forth. Restricting the number of electives and tying them to a particular grade level facilitates this process. It may be necessary to pair electives so that students scheduled into one are automatically scheduled into another. Also, requiring all students to take one particular elective, such as physical education, greatly reduces conflicts, as student placement then is determined by one elective instead of two. For example, if all students scheduled into electives first period are placed on a team, these students then take physical education during the other teacher conference period.

Still another approach to scheduling teams is to hand schedule each student or groups of students. Although this is routine in small districts, some larger districts find this to be the most efficient method for scheduling teams, particularly when there are numerous conflicts. Sometimes giving a group of teachers time to perform this duty brings results with which the staff is most satisfied.

Scheduling teams of students with a small group of teachers is often problematic and, of the various scheduling models, can present the most difficulties. For some schools, beginning by forming only one team the first year and subsequently adding others is more manageable. Other schools limit teaming to only a few subjects. Blocking a group of students for two periods with two teachers is fairly easy within a traditional model and still provides teachers considerable instructional freedom. As with any other model, the advantages to teachers and students have to be weighed in light of scheduling feasibility.

Whatever the model and the process, finding a schedule that works best for teachers and students is the goal. Once the schedule is implemented, problems, complaints, and satisfaction with the schedule during the school are noted by the principal. This information becomes the basis for improving the schedule the following year. Thus, over time, teacher, pupil, and parent satisfaction with how time is spent at school is increased.

REFERENCES

Hanson, B. (1996). *McGraw-Hill School Systems' master schedule building workshop manual.* Monterey, CA.

Merenbloom, E. Y. (1991). *The team process.* Columbus, OH: National Middle School Association.

CHAPTER 5

Flexible Scheduling for Elementary Schools

> *When the voices of children are heard on the green*
> *And laughing is heard on the hill,*
> *My heart is at rest within my breast*
> *And everything else is still.*
> —William Blake

While many of the scheduling considerations previously described for middle schools are also applicable to elementary schools, unique challenges exist for administrators of students in the early grades. Young students have short attention spans, need strong relationships with adults and require close monitoring. The range of maturity levels in students between kindergarten and fifth or sixth grades is broader than between sixth and eighth or ninth and twelfth graders. Although the principal usually has less direct involvement in the hour-by-hour scheduling of students' time as teachers are told when special classes such as physical education are to be held and teachers are free to determine how the rest of the day is spent, when and where young children engage in physical activity is important to them and to their learning. The purpose of this chapter is to address the singular characteristics of the elementary school environment and their influence on scheduling. This chapter is supplemental to Chapters 1, 2, and 3, rather than in place of them.

A RATIONALE FOR CHANGE AT THE ELEMENTARY LEVEL

Flexible scheduling in the elementary school is not a new concept. In-

This chapter is coauthored by Paul Terry and Gwen Schroth.

spired by the reform movement of the nineties that focused on the learner-centered school, elementary educators have been searching for methods to enhance student learning. Among the innovations attracting attention is the provision of sufficient blocks of time for elementary students to learn in authentic and purposeful ways, for example, through parallel block scheduling. By partitioning the school day into longer chunks of time and providing teachers more flexibility in how they use that time, elementary school faculties can create a framework that favors the needs of the learner rather than focusing on the needs of the school organization. Young children need time for teacher–student and student–student relationships to develop; time for play; time for physical involvement with the learning; time for a wide variety of activities, some of short duration; and time to make connections between subject matter and their own world. These student needs occur in unpredictable order, and the time required to meet these needs varies from day to day and even hour to hour. Teachers must have the flexibility to change what students do and for how long they do it.

The traditional elementary schedule breaks the day into small segments of time where every subject is addressed daily, but are interrupted when students, as a group, are assigned to physical education, music, or art classes. In addition, the regular classroom schedule may be disrupted when individual or small groups of students leave for special services, such as special education or gifted programs. Title 1 Programs, federally funded to provide supplemental instruction for low achieving, disadvantaged students, are frequently scheduled so that students come and go at the request of the Title 1 teachers, further disrupting classroom instruction. These breaks in academic time are generally planned by someone else, yet the teacher must adjust the classroom schedule accordingly.

While the school principal is in charge of scheduling when teachers take their students from their classroom to music, art, or physical education, the order in which other subjects are scheduled and the amount of time allowed for each is often decided by the grade level team or individual teacher. Each day's schedule looks much like every other day.

Traditional scheduling in elementary schools does create administrative problems for principals. For example:

(1) Teachers tend to feel that every student must have their reading and/or math class in the morning, before lunch, when the students are thought to be more alert. Teachers resent interruptions during that time for special classes such as physical education.

(2) Teachers frequently feel entitled to having specialists teach music, art, and physical education and have strong preferences about the day and time when these are scheduled.
(3) Special programs such as Title 1 or special education services often require individual students or small groups to leave class, disrupting the continuity of classroom instruction.
(4) Resentment builds when specialists have lower teacher–pupil ratios than regular classroom teachers.
(5) Students in the early grades need morning and afternoon recess times for physical activity, and these must be coordinated so playgrounds do not become overcrowded.
(6) After lunch, nap time should be built into the schedule for all-day kindergarten students.
(7) Planning periods, computer laboratory time, music, art, and lunch must be coordinated for the entire school. Teachers have preferences about when and how often these occur and can feel slighted if their wishes are not considered.
(8) Lunch must be scheduled so that children do not eat too early or too late in the day.
(9) In smaller districts, specialists such as music, art, and special education teachers are shared by several campuses, and principals may have little influence over these scheduling decisions although they impact each school's schedule.

Innovative scheduling can solve some of these problems. A wise administrator carefully considers all alternatives before making scheduling decisions.

THE CASE FOR LONGER CLASS PERIODS

Throughout America, talk of restructuring schools is popular. The National Association of Secondary School Principals (NASSP) calls restructuring the newest and most profound word in the educator's dictionary (1992). Although this word has lacked a clear definition and varies from group to group, NASSP states its position clearly. Schools, including those for small children, must change if the social and economic problems facing our country are to be appropriately addressed.

After more than a decade of educational restructuring and reform, most observers agree that many aspects of restructuring have dealt more with administrative structures and policy-making processes than with specific, meaningful changes in the way teachers teach and students learn. Many educators would agree with Sizer (1992) that the reform movement largely avoids the real world found inside the schools and that there is no stomach to accept the hard reality that the ways Americans keep their schools are sadly misdirected.

Against this backdrop, however, educational historians of the future may discover that a true signal of meaningful education reform occurred with the publication of the *1994 Report of the National Education Commission on Time and Learning,* which stated:

> If experience, research, and common sense teach nothing else, they confirm the truism that people learn at different rates, and in different ways with different subjects. But we put the cart before the horse: our schools and the people involved with them—students, parents, teachers, administrators, and staff—are captives of clock and calendar. The boundaries of student growth are defined by schedules for bells, buses, and vacations instead of standards for students and learning. (p. 7)

Elementary schools typically reflect the secondary, six- to eight-period days without questioning the value of such time frames. In discussing the six-period day, the National Education Commission on Time and Learning (1994) reported that, no matter how complex or simple the school subject—reading, mathematics, language arts, science, social studies, art, music, or physical education—the typical schedule assigns each an impartial national average of 51 minutes per subject per day, regardless of how well or poorly students comprehend the material.

We do know that elementary children have short attention spans and their memories are not yet fully developed, making 50 to 60 minutes per subject totally inappropriate for some children for some subjects (see Chapter 1, Responding to Student Needs).

The Commission's findings show that the school schedule governs how administrators organize the school and how teachers work their way through the curriculum. Above all else, it governs how material is presented to the students and the opportunity they have to comprehend and master it. One might conclude that the traditional elementary schedule of dividing subject matter into small portions of 30- to 50-minute time periods might have been arrived at over the years as the maximum length of time a typical elementary teacher could teach and students could endure!

The necessity for education reformers to explore change in terms of time and learning is supported by the Commission's conclusion that the whole question of teachers and time needs to be seriously and systematically rethought. The issue is not simply teachers. It is not just time. The real issue is education quality. Teachers need time to develop effective lessons, assess students, and discuss the results with students individually. They need time to listen to students, particularly at the elementary level where student–teacher relationships are so crucial. They need time to read professional journals, interact with colleagues, and watch outstanding teachers demonstrate new strategies.

In response to the need for more innovative models, some elementary schools are moving from the traditional "bell schedule" to more flexible formats, for example, the block schedule where periods are redesigned into 90, 120, and even 220 blocks of undisturbed time. As advocated by Goodlad (1984) in *A Place Called School: Prospects for the Future,* the concept of block scheduling is rooted in concerns about creating sufficient time to immerse elementary students in the learning experience. Block scheduling at the elementary level is about teacher teams, clusters of students, and time to plan and learn.

Plans that provide for longer class periods hold great potential for redesigning the traditional elementary school day into a meaningful instructional system. Flexible scheduling, whether it is block or some variation thereof, provides a variety of advantages that directly influence the quality of student instruction.

For teachers, longer class periods

- allow for a wide variety of activities centered around one learning concept with large and small groups, depending on instructional and student needs
- facilitate team teaching
- enhance development of interdisciplinary units
- allow time for field trips
- encourage cooperative, creative teaching strategies

For students, longer learning periods

- are less disruptive
- allow for transfer of learning when subject areas are integrated
- provide time for establishing relationships with peers and teachers

Redistribution of teachers so that teacher–pupil ratios are more equitable is also possible when scheduling is less traditional. In the recent report of the National Commission on Teaching and America's Future (1996), one of the five major recommendations was to create schools that are organized for student and teacher success. The report intimated that our schools are bureaucratic inheritances from the nineteenth century, noting that the allocation of teachers in some schools with a pupil–teacher ratio of only thirteen to one regular class sizes averaged twenty-three and went as high as thirty-three, because of the assignment of many staff to pull-out and specialist positions.

Class sizes can drop to about fourteen in elementary schools by bringing specialists to the students in the classroom rather than using pull-out arrangements, which allows teachers to keep students in regular classrooms. According to the report of the National Commission on Teaching and America's Future (1996), some elementary schools have already implemented this strategy by teaming regular and special education teachers with a group of students during long blocks of time.

The major hurdle innovative scheduling presents at the elementary level is that change is mandatory. For innovation to be effective, the school principal must know how to engage the faculty in the change process and what to do to optimize the chances for success. Chapter 2 of this book provides specific guidelines for leading schools through the change process.

FLEXIBLE SCHEDULING AT THE ELEMENTARY LEVEL

Parallel Block Scheduling

One method for block scheduling at the elementary level that has been found to be effective is parallel block scheduling, an innovation that is being used in more than fifty schools nationwide (Canady & Fogliani, 1989; Canady, 1990). For parallel scheduling, during critical reading and math instruction, each teacher at the same grade level or different grade levels works with two groups. During the first portion of the blocked instructional period, one group is receiving teacher-led instruction. The second group moves either to another classroom for support services such as special education, Title 1, and gifted and talented or to an instructional area known as an "extension center" for a variety of enrichment activities. Extension activities can include computer laboratories, independent reading, problem solving, creative writing, science experiments, or literature appreciation. Extension activities can occur in the library, cafeteria, or in an extra classroom. During the second portion of the time block, the two groups change places.

This arrangement allows instruction to occur continually for all students, significantly increasing the total amount of teacher-directed instruction. Parallel blocking is in contrast to what would normally take place in a typical elementary classroom of twenty-five students. While most students are at their seats completing written assignments, the teacher is working with a small group at a table. One of the primary advantages of the parallel block schedule is decreased disruption for both the students and the teacher during the direct instructional periods. This particular method can be used within grade levels as well as with several grade levels.

Canady (1990) lists a number of advantages to parallel block scheduling.

(1) For students,
- Most of the day is spent in mixed, heterogeneous groups.
- Homogeneous grouping is possible in mathematics, reading, and special education.
- Small-group instructional time may be increased.
- Instructional periods are not disrupted by pull-out programs.
- Unsupervised seat work time is reduced.

(2) For teachers
- Opportunities to capitalize on teacher strengths are provided.
- Small groups allow teacher–student relationships to be strengthened.
- Pull-out programs are coordinated with classroom activity.
- Dependency or basal material and "locked-in" groups can be reduced.

(3) For the school,
- Additional staff or funding may not be required.
- Cooperative efforts between staff members are increased.

An important premise of block scheduling is that it provides a framework for allowing teachers time to give their students more personalized attention. Carl Rogers (as cited by Black, Puckett, & Bell, 1992) states that elementary teachers are significant adults in children's lives and establishing strong relationships is important for students' growth.

Disadvantages to block scheduling must also be considered.

(1) For teachers,

- Change always involves some level of stress and requires time for successful implementation.
- Altered instructional methods are required.
- Additional planning time is necessary during transition.
- Control over students engaged outside the classroom may be lost.

(2) For students,
- Change to unfamiliar extension activities may be difficult.
- Increased independence is required when moving from one setting to another.
- Security of staying with one teacher and the same peers all day is lost. This is a serious disadvantage for students who lack the independence to function well in a variety of settings.

(3) For schools,
- More dollars may be required for staffing and, as teachers become more creative with teaching time, additional resources may be needed.

Considering the overload some teachers experience in traditional classrooms and the amount of time many students spend sitting quietly conducting seat work, parallel block scheduling certainly merits consideration. Teachers who understand the concept and make full use of its benefits are likely to find such a model beneficial.

Other Flexible Scheduling Models

While block scheduling is a popular scheduling innovation available to elementary principals wishing to maximize the use of students' time, other alternatives are possible if administrators are willing to spend time with their faculties, exploring solutions to key problems.

FLEXIBLY SCHEDULING SPECIAL PROGRAMS

One of the most common problems facing elementary teachers is dealing with students' fragmented daily schedules. While special services are worthwhile, classroom teachers feel frustrated when students come and go from their classrooms throughout the day. Some students miss the regular classroom instruction when they attend Title 1 or gifted programs, instruction that must fit into some other part of their day. If a number of students attend special programs, coordinating each student's instructional needs can be difficult. While parallel block scheduling is one solution, a modified form of that format is also possible.

For this author, solving the problem of fragmented schedules due to special programs became a priority in one school. As elementary principal, faculty discussions disclosed that grades three, four, and five had many more students being pulled from the classroom for special services such as Title 1, special education, gifted and talented, and band than did grades one and two. The faculty decided to divide the school day into large blocks of time and assign each grade a 90-minute time block during which all non-classroom instructional activities took place. Figure 5.1 shows this configuration.

The most difficult task for the faculty was breaking away from traditional modes of thinking about elementary scheduling. One question that had to be addressed was whether or not all grade levels need the same amount of time in such activities as music, physical education, and art. The advantages of the agreed upon schedule were

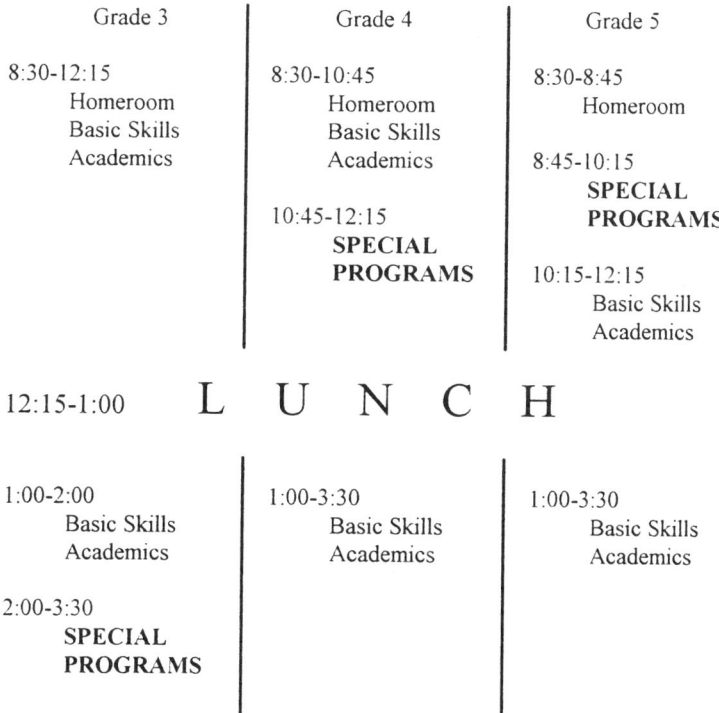

Figure 5.1 Flexible scheduling: special programs.

- in-depth student learning, for example, from simulations, group work, debates, outdoor study, and lab work
- variety in assessment strategies
- intense focus on basic skills
- individualized instruction
- decreased student frustration
- reduced discipline problems in hallways as students were not coming and going throughout the entire day
- facilitation of team teaching and interdisciplinary units

USING TITLE 1 TO ADVANTAGE

Title 1 is a federally funded program whose goal is improving instruction for disadvantaged students. In schools where most students qualify for Title 1 services, all students are allowed to take advantage of the program, creating possibilities for flexible scheduling. To use Title 1 to teachers' and students' advantage, all students are grouped as high and low achievers. At one such school, each grade level has seven sections with twenty-eight students in each section. The school arranges its Title 1 funds to provide two Title 1 teachers for each grade level. As shown in Figure 5.2, the Title 1 teachers meet with groups of students on alternating schedules addressing reading, language arts, spelling, and some math concepts. This model allows low achieving students to remain in the regular classroom on some days, rather than being removed from their peers daily. When the low achieving students leave from Title 1 instruction, the regular classroom teacher is able to work with the remaining, smaller group of students.

Additional Strategies

Decisions regarding scheduling are typically made by the school administrator. When lunch periods, physical education, and music are held is more often than not out of teachers' control. Teachers must be involved in scheduling. One strategy is the team concept. A team of teachers, representing the various grade levels, can work with the principal on scheduling. Of critical importance is having special area teachers included on this planning team.

Starting with the previous year's schedule, problems are identified and corrected. For example, if teachers find physical education disruptive to reading and math classes in the morning, P.E. may have to be

	Week A	
	Monday/ Wednesday/ Friday	Tuesday/ Thursday
8:45-9:30	Ms. May's Higher achieving students	Ms. May's Lower achieving students
9:30-10:15	Mr. Dunn's Higher achieving students	Mr. Dunn's Lower achieving students
10:15-11:45	Planning, Conferencing, Lunch	
11:45-12:30	Ms. Zerbe's Higher achieving students	Ms. Zerbe's Lower achieving students
12:30-1:15	Ms. Schweer's Higher achieving students	Ms. Schweer's Lower achieving students
1:15-2:30	Planning	
2:30-3:00	Non Readers for additional services for 9 weeks followed by enrichment for highest achievers for 9 weeks	

Week B

Higher achieving students follow the Tuesday/ Thursday schedule. Lower achieving students follow the Monday/ Wedenesday/ Friday schedule.

Figure 5.2 A Title 1 teacher's schedule: first grade.

rotated yearly among the grades to demonstrate equity. If playground areas are limited, the team can cooperatively work out recess schedules that best fit each teacher's needs.

Teachers can also agree to schedule reading and mathematics at the same time of day throughout the school to facilitate grouping across classrooms and grade levels. This modified block scheduling concept provides flexibility for students and encourages teachers to work together creatively.

GUIDELINES FOR BLOCK SCHEDULING

Hackman (1995) proposes ten excellent guidelines to be used by administrators and faculty for implementing block scheduling. The guidelines are general enough to be applied to most innovative scheduling arrangements at the elementary level. Hackman encourages a collaborative approach to school reform.

(1) Employ a systems thinking approach. Empower the faculty by providing opportunities for significant input into the schedule and its interrelated parts, guided by the fundamental principle of what is best for students. Assigning an advisory team made up of teachers from each grade level and from special services is one example of a systems approach at the elementary level.

(2) Secure the support of superiors. Changing from traditional schedules may affect areas beyond the jurisdiction of the principal and faculty. Additions or reductions in staff and budget concerns definitely involve the central administration's input or approval. As most districts have more than one elementary school, providing additional resources for one may create a demand from other elementary principals for equal advantages, a demand central administrators and boards may not wish to meet.

(3) Understand the change process. As outlined in Chapter 2, change is complicated, and, for true success, requires careful attention. For example, teachers require appropriate staff development to peruse and review all alternative models of scheduling as well as creating their own. Teachers cannot be expected to use the same teaching strategies and/or techniques when moving to longer periods of time. The reader is advised to read Chapter 2 carefully before considering any innovation.

(4) Involve all stakeholders. Hackman postulates that building principals have three critical functions when it comes to change: (a) to ensure that all interested parties are involved: (b) to explain the rationale for change to the school board, central office adminstration, teachers, parents, and students; and (c) to actively support teachers as they struggle with the demands of changing their instructional methods. Explaining the rationale for an innovation to the community-at-large is also wise. This can be accomplished by involving the media through news coverage in the local newspaper or local television station about how the changes will benefit students. Many stakeholders in the community do not have young school-age children; however, they do support the public school through tax contributions. Therefore, any negative information via teachers, parents, or those intimately involved with the school can be negated by positive media coverage.

(5) Consult sources outside the school. Numerous resources are available when considering schedule changes in an elementary school, for example, journal articles, videotapes, state and national conferences, and invited educators who have implemented block schedules can come and speak candidly about barriers to change. Particularly effective is taking groups of teachers to visit other schools where major change has been successful. These schools may exist within the district when there are several elementary schools and should not be overlooked as a resource.

(6) Brainstorm creative alternatives. Instead of focusing on implementing a new schedule or attempting to adopt another school's model, the faculty needs the opportunity to brainstorm what they would like to do that the current schedule does not allow. Elementary teachers may be more reticent than secondary teachers when it comes to voicing opinions, and the principal may need to draw them out, making sure that the climate is safe for voicing concerns.

(7) Examine the budgetary implications. Although additional funding may not be needed, assess monetary needs not only from the personnel perspective, but also in terms of resources and materials. With instruction taught in longer blocks and the possibility opened up for interdisciplinary teaming, teachers are likely to become creative and require new materials as they move away from standard practices. Creativity require risks, so the principal should be open to experimentation and not get discouraged when some ventures fail.

(8) Plan faculty inservice. Prepare the faculty/staff and any other interested parties by allowing them to select topics of interest to them during both the planning and implementation stages of change. Staff development must be appropriate for elementary level teachers, rather than "piggy-backing" on secondary or training generic to all levels.

Hackman cautions that we must prepare for the "implementation dip" that will most likely occur, recognizing that things may briefly get worse before they get better. Teachers should be aware of such a possibility. They should also have the opportunity to rely upon their collective expertise in lesson development. To adjust to longer instructional periods, such collaboration may be helpful.

(9) Include an evaluation component. The faculty must identify in-

dicators they want to use to evaluate the new schedule's effectiveness. By determining the indicators prior to implementing the schedule, baseline data should be collected. For elementary schools, building-wide measures can include student discipline referrals, attendance data, grades, standardized test scores, honor roll data, self-esteem indicators, and feedback from teachers and parents. Observing small children's ability to move from setting to setting is key to evaluating the program. Some evaluations may show immediate results, while others, such as student achievement, will have to be tracked over several years.

(10) Share successes. While faculty morale may decline the first year of implementation, building a climate of care and concern can keep them on track. Sharing positive results as well as frustrations can help build such a climate. The building principal should take every opportunity to publicly praise the faculty for their hard work, courage, and tenacity in wanting to improve for the benefit of the students.

Elementary principals, together with their faculties, need to explore all possible avenues for improving how students' and teachers' time is spent. Flexible scheduling offers only one method for making the most of the precious hours children spend at school. Principals who convey the message that how time is spent is of utmost importance are setting high expectations for teachers and, in turn, for students. Because time is a limited resource, scheduling how that resource will be used is critical. Schedule for learning, not for convenience.

REFERENCES

Black, J. K., Puckett, M. B., & Bell, M. J. (1992). *The young child: Development from prebirth through age eight.* New York: Merrill Publishing Company.

Canady, R. L. (1990). A better way to organize a school. *Principal, 69*(3), 34–36.

Canady, R. L., & Fogliani, A. E. (1989, August). How to cut class size. *The Executive Educator, 11*(8), 22–23.

Conely, D. T. (1993). Restructuring in search of a definition. *Principal, 72*(3), 13–15.

Goodlad, J. (1984). *A place called school: Prospects for the future.* New York: McGraw-Hill Publishing Company.

Hackman, D. (1995). Ten guidelines for implementing block scheduling. *Educational Leadership, 53*(3), 24–27.

National Association of Secondary School Principals' Commission on Restructuring (1992). *A leader's guide to school restructuring.* Reston, Virginia: NASSP.

National Commission on Teaching and America's Future (1996). *What matters most: Teaching for America's future.* Washington, DC: Government Printing Office.

National Education Commission on Time and Learning (1994). *Prisoners of time.* Washington, DC: Government Printing Office.

Sizer, T. R. (1992). *Horaces' school: Redesigning the American high school.* Boston: Houghton Mifflin Company.

APPENDIX A

Computer Programs

A number of computer programs are designed to meet a variety of school districts' needs such as business, accounting, student records, and scheduling. In some states, regional service centers provide computer services with scheduling as one program among many. The computer programs listed in this section have features provided specifically for scheduling.

EDUSOLVE

EduSolve is a program designed for use with either IBM or Macintosh computers and is a multi-user system. Specific hardware and networking requirements depend on school size and the number of nodes on the network. The system accommodates large numbers of students and can schedule blocked times, teaming, and traditional plans. Via the Internet, parents are able to view their child's schedule, grades, and report cards. Among other services, EduSolve can

- create a master schedule
- build students' schedules
- prioritize students as designated
- write student four-year plans
- print a variety of reports
- create a conflict matrix
- schedule multiple lunch periods

For further information, contact EduSolve Corporation, 3624 Oak Lawn Avenue, Suite 100, Dallas, TX 75219; Phone: 214-526-2991; Fax: 214-526-5295; e-mail: info@edusolve.com; Web site: http://www.edusolve.com.

MAC SCHOOL

Mac School Student Information System operates on the Apple Macintosh family of computers and includes a multi-user system. Specific hardware and networking requirements depend on school size and the number of nodes on the network. A complete Mac School line provides central office personnel with student, teacher, and course information, an accounting system, and library program. It can schedule a maximum of 5,000 students in 2,000 classes. Accommodating rotating, modular, traditional schedules, the program is suitable for year-round, year-long, semester, and 6- or 9-week courses. Among its capabilities, Mac School can

- build the master schedule
- print student schedules
- scan student course requests
- update class rosters
- prioritize students as designated
- schedule for team teaching
- define the relationship between groups of courses
- create a conflict matrix
- balance class sections
- lock in classes that have constraints
- schedule multiple lunch periods
- print a large variety of reports

For more information on this program, contact Chancery Software Ltd., 2211 Rimland Drive, #224, Bellingham, WA 98226; phone: 800-999-9931, or 206-738-3211; Fax: 206-738-3255.

MACRO EDUCATIONAL SYSTEMS, INC.

Macro Educational Systems, Inc. offers two scheduling programs: School Administrative Student Information (SASI) III and SASIxp. They are district-wide integrated systems for use on Windows, Macintosh, and Power PC.

SASIxp

SASIxp is an upgraded version of SASI III and includes grade reporting, progress files, course and test history for individual students, attendance, and special education, as well as scheduling. Among the scheduling features is the ability to

- assign large groups of students
- scan course requests
- print a conflict matrix
- analyze and re-attempt rejects
- print reports

- accommodate a wide variety of block formats
- schedule periods at different times of day, by cycle chosen
- list partially scheduled students

SASI III

- balance classes by race and ethnicity
- list open periods in student schedules
- list partially scheduled students
- print a conflict matrix
- mass change course requests
- analyze class loads
- print reports
- scan requests

For further information, contact Macro Educational Systems, 23461 South Pointe Drive, Suite 200, Laguna Hills, CA 92653-1523; Phone: 714-768-6000; Fax: 714-586-3255.

McGRAW-HILL SCHOOL SYSTEMS

McGraw-Hill provides a number of programs for Windows or DOS. Some programs are available on Apple and Macintosh platforms. Other McGraw-Hill packages include finance, student information, grading, skill tracking, and test scoring. The School System and Osiris, a DOS-based software system, manage student information, discipline, demographics, health, enrollment, scheduling, attendance, and grade reporting. These systems integrate with district-level and classroom systems for sharing purposes. The capabilities of the School System and Osiris include the following:

- schedule up to four semesters including quarter and full-year courses
- reschedule students
- schedule basic courses before electives
- accept all types of schedules
- scan requests
- adhere to course-section preferences
- balance classes by demographic fields

McGraw-Hill also markets The Elementary School System (TESS). This program includes student records, attendance, grade reporting, and student scheduling. Modules can be added for fee accounting, networking to unlimited workstations, exchanging data with a central site, and building reports.

For further information, contact McGraw-Hill School Systems, 20

Ryan Ranch Road, Monterey, CA 93940; Phone: 800-663-0544; http://www.mhss.com.

Another important service provided by McGraw-Hill is a scheduling workshop conducted across the country by Mr. Bob Hanson. The workshop is designed for new schedulers at the middle and high school levels. For information, call McGraw-Hill or Mr. Hanson at 319-351-5104.

THE MODULAR MANAGEMENT SYSTEM FOR SCHOOLS

The MMS: Student Scheduling System provides an integrated scheduling system that can be run on Windows, Macintosh, and DOS or Unix. It can accommodate standard, rotating, team, block, alternate week schedules in elementary, middle or high schools. Scheduling for a full year, by semester, quarters, trimesters, or six-terms, it also provides student attendance, grades, and discipline records. Among other capabilities, the complete package can

- build a master schedule
- optimize seating among sections
- prioritize courses scheduled
- create a conflict matrix
- scan student registration forms
- balance enrollment between semesters and within departments
- allow course limitations
- create student and teacher schedules

MMS: Student Scheduling System is available from Computer Resources, Inc., Rte. 125, P.O. Box 60, Barrington, NH 03825; Phone: 603-664-5811; Fax: 603-664-5864; e-mail: sales@cri-mms.com.

NATIONAL COMPUTER SYSTEMS, INC.

NCS offers Comprehensive Information Management for Schools III (CIMS III), designed to utilize the integrated, relational database of the IBM AS/400 mid-range computer family accessed via attached personal computers or standard terminals. Software is available for Windows. Assessment, instruction, finance, and human resource accounting packages are at hand. Among its capabilities, CIMS III can

- help build a master schedule
- balance by number, sex, race, ethnicity, grade, and student group
- scan requests
- print a conflict matrix
- link courses

- select alternate courses
- schedule student groups
- print reports
- schedule mosiac and modular formats

Obtain more information from National Computer Systems, Inc., 11000 Prairie Lakes Drive, Eden Prairie, MN 55344; Phone: 800-447-3269; Fax: 612-893-8102.

SOFTWARE TECHNOLOGY INC.

STI offers the Student Scheduling and Tracking System (SSTS) 2000 for Windows or DOS, which includes scheduling, grading, attendance, discipline tracking, instructional management functions, textbook management, and complete transcript tracking. Among other features, SSTS 2000 can

- build the schedule
- schedule for more than 1 year
- accommodate alternate-day, block scheduling
- balance classes across and within semesters
- print reports
- scan requests
- list partially scheduled students
- balance classes by race and sex

For further information, contact Software Technology Inc., 1110 Montlimar Drive, Suite 150, Mobile, AL 36609-1721; Phone: 205-344-7600 or 800-844-0884.

THE SURFSIDE SOLUTION III

Surfside Solution III is intended for use in an IBM or MS-DOS compatible personal computer with 2 megabytes RAM, at least one diskette drive, a hard disk, and an 80 column printer. A network version is also available. The module is intended for use in a one-day cycle school with up to sixteen periods in the day. It can schedule approximately 2,500 students at one time and accommodate 500 different courses. The module also provides such services as attendance and grading. Among other capabilities, the program is able to

- construct a master schedule
- set sections, meeting lengths, and semesters
- build a preliminary schedule
- create teacher and student schedules

- add and drop students
- enter/edit student requests
- schedule singletons without conflict
- count students requesting each section
- generate a conflict matrix

Further information on this program can be obtained from Surfside Software, Inc., P.O. Box 1112, 79 Finlay Road, East Orleans, MA 02643; Phone: 800-942-9008; 508-255-1120; Fax: 508-255-9520.

TEXAS EDUCATIONAL CONSULTATIVE SERVICES, INC.

TECS software is designed to work with IBM's System/36 and AD/400 hardware platforms. The IBM mid-range hardware platforms allow a district to maintain all data on one machine, while providing access at various campuses through attached personal computers or terminals. Software is available for additional services such as payroll, general ledger, personnel, budget, fixed assets, student accounting, discipline, and special education. Among other features, TECS software can

- scan student requests
- define scheduling order
- schedule groups by sex or grade
- schedule teams
- schedule for 2 years or semesters
- bridge a period across semesters
- construct reports

For further information, contact TECS, P.O. Box 18898, Austin, TX 78760; Phone: 512-443-4433; Fax: 512-443-0586.

WIN SCHOOL INFORMATION SYSTEM

Win School is a Windows-based program produced by Chancery Software Ltd. The computer choice depends on whether a single district requires a user system or multi-user (networked) system. Memory required depends on database and storage size. The system stores information on 5,000 students in as many as 2,000 classes as well as student records, ethnic category, home language, and team/club memberships. The program is suitable for year-round schools, year-long, semester, and 6- or 9-week courses and can accommodate a variety of course structures, for example, classes that do not meet daily. Discipline records, report cards, and attendance are other capabilities. The Win School is able to

- build the master schedule
- print student schedules
- scan student course requests
- update class rosters
- prioritize students as requested
- schedule for team teaching
- create a conflict matrix
- balance class sections
- lock in classes with constraints
- accommodate multiple lunch schedules
- print a large variety of reports

For more information on this program, contact Chancery Software Ltd., 2211 Rimland Drive, #224, Bellingham, WA 98226; Phone: 800-999-9931 or 206-738-3211; Fax: 206-738-3255.

REFERENCES

Chancery Software Ltd. (1996). *WinSchool* (Brochure). Bellingham, WA.
Chancery Software Ltd. (1994). *Mac school* (Brochure). Bellingham, WA.
Computer Resources, Inc. (1994). *Modular management system for schools* (Brochure). Barrington, NH.
EduSolve (1996). *Advance solutions for school management* (Brochure). Dallas, TX.
Macro Educational Systems, Inc. (1996). *SASIxp mass scheduling training guide* (Brochure). Laguna Hills, CA.
McGraw-Hill School Systems (1996). *The school system* (Brochure). Monterey, CA.
National Computing Systems, Inc. (1995). *NCS comprehensive information management for schools III* (Brochure). Minneapolis, MN.
Software Technology, Inc. (1996). *The student scheduling and tracking system* (Brochure). Mobile, AL.
Surfside Software, Inc. (1995). *The surfside solution III schedule module for IBM compatible computers* (Brochure). East Orleans, MA.
Texas Educational Consultative Services, Inc. (1996). *Scheduling software* (Brochure). Austin, TX.

APPENDIX B

Frequently Asked Questions

Administrators new to scheduling and those contemplating new scheduling formats have many questions. Among those frequently asked are the following.

(1) Where do you start with scheduling?
Response: Chapter 4 outlines the precise steps for creating a master schedule, including a suggested timeline that delineates activities to begin in January and end when schedules are distributed.

(2) How much flexibility is there in the schedule once it is adopted?
Response: The master schedule can be changed at any time, but changing the schedule always impacts a number of students, either positively or negatively. Changes are not advisable once school begins.

(3) On what basis and when should students be allowed to change their schedules?
Response: School guidelines should be made public and state when schedules can be changed (for example, the first 2 weeks of school) and when changes will no longer be considered.

(4) How are classes balanced by gender, race, and student ability, and is there a computer program available to do that for the scheduler?
Response: Most computer scheduling programs can balance classes (see the computer programs listed in the Appendix A).

(5) Should the principal honor parent requests for a particular teacher for their child?
Response: This is an administrative decision but should be fair to all students. In some states, principals are required to honor one such parent request each year.

(6) How much and in what way should teachers be involved in creating the master schedule? How do you seek the support of your staff when adopting a new scheduling format?
Response: Chapter 2 addresses staff involvement as a change issue, and

Chapter 3 discusses the need for staff involvement and ways in which teachers can contribute to creating a successful schedule.

(7) How do you handle scheduling teachers' conference periods given that some teachers have strong preferences?

Response: Conference period assignments can create conflict among and between teachers and the principal. Chapter 3 addresses this issue in more detail.

(8) What electives should be offered?

Response: The middle school concept calls for exposing students to as many different electives as possible. The number of electives a school is able to actually offer is constrained by the number of teachers the district is able to afford. Remember, the electives determine the number of students each teacher will have each period. Students must be placed somewhere each period so, when too few electives are available for one period, more students must be placed in regular classes during that time.

(9) How many minutes do students need to pass from one class to another?

Response: The length of passing periods is partially determined by the time it takes students to get from one class to another, which is a function of the size of the school. The other consideration is how much time is to be allowed for visiting lockers and restrooms and for students to socialize.

(10) How is computer-assisted instruction worked into the schedule?

Response: Computer-assisted instruction that takes place outside the regular teacher's classroom should be scheduled by the computer instructor together with classroom teachers with the advice of the adminstrator. Sometimes, computer laboratory instruction is targeted at low achievers, but time for high achieving students is allotted before and after school and during periods when the laboratory is not in use (for example, when the instructor has lunch or a planning period).

(11) Once a master schedule is created, can the same schedule be used the following year?

Response: By all means, once a workable schedule is created, it can be used again. Each year, minor changes can clear up problem areas. The major variable is the number of students requesting a course, which can change the number of sections scheduled. If students are grouped by ability, teachers may want to make yearly changes to the levels they teach.

(12) How is the number of students in each class determined?

Response: As discussed in Chapter 4, the administrator, together with the teachers, should decide the maximum number of students allowed in each class. The number of students actually scheduled is determined when students' requests for courses are processed by the computer, resulting in some classes having smaller numbers than others.

(13) What computer programs are available for scheduling?

Response: Appendix A provides a listing of some of the computer programs available for scheduling and outlines some of the advantages of each.

(14) What guidelines form the basis for grouping students by ability?
Response: Ability grouping is discussed in Chapter 3. While research on grouping should be considered when making such decisions, parent pressures may require a minimum of grouping. Teacher recommendations and test scores are generally used for determining placement by ability.

(15) Should our school adopt the blocked scheduling format?
Response: The choice of scheduling format, be it teaming, block, or traditional scheduling, should reflect the needs of the students. Chapter 2 discusses change issues, and Chapter 3 outlines the advantages and disadvantages of each type of scheduling.

(16) How are students assigned to teams when teaming is adopted?
Response: Students can be assigned to interest, ability, electives, race, and gender, depending on the intent of the grouping. Chapters 3 and 4 address this problem.

(17) What scheduling resources should the principal ask of the school district?
Response: An administrator should expect the district to provide adequate staffing to complete student schedules on time and to provide a computer program that best meets the school's needs.

(18) How are schedules determined on early release days?
Response: Sometimes the last period of the day is eliminated from the schedule for early release days, but teachers may prefer that all classes meet for a short period of time. Another option is to rotate the period that is eliminated so that one class is not missed too frequently.

BIBLIOGRAPHY

Beggs, D. W. III. (1984). *A practical application of the Trump Plan.* Englewood Cliffs, NJ: Prentice-Hall.

Belasco, J. A. (1990). *Teaching the elephant to dance: Empowering change in your organization.* New York: Crown Publishers, Inc.

Belasco, J. A. & Stayer, R. C. (1993). *Flight of the buffalo: Soaring to excellence, learning to let employees lead.* New York: Warner.

Bennis, W., & Nanus, B. (1985). *Leaders: Strategies for taking charge.* New York: Harper and Row.

Black, J. K., Puckett, M. B., & Bell, M. J. (1982). *The young child: Development from prebirth through age eight.* New York: Merrill Publishing Company.

Boyd, V. (1992). *School context: Bridge or barrier to change?* Austin, TX: Southwest Educational Development Laboratory.

Bridges, W. (1991). *Managing transitions: Making the most of change.* Reading, MA: Addison-Wesley.

Brophy, G. (1992). Probing the subtleties of subject-matter teaching. *Educational Leadership, 49*(7), 4–7.

Canady, R. L., & Fogliani. (1989, August). How to cut class size. *The Executive Educator, 11*(8), 22–23.

Canady, R. L., & Rettig, M. D. (1992). Restructuring middle level schedules to promote equal access. *Schools in the Middle, 1*(4), 20–26.

Canady, R. L. & Rettig, M. D. (1993, December). Unlocking the lockstep high school schedule. *Phi Delta Kappan, 75*(4), 310–314.

Carnegie Council on Adolescent Development. (1989). *Turning points: Preparing American youth for the 21st century. The report of the task force on education of young adolescents.* New York: Carnegie Council on Adolescent Development.

Chancery Software Ltd. (1996). *WinSchool* (Brochure). Bellingham, WA.

Chancery Software Ltd. (1994). *Mac school* (Brochure). Bellingham, WA.

Computer Resources, Inc. (1994). *Modular management system for schools* (Brochure). Barrington, NH.

Conely, D. T. (1993). Restructuring in search of a definition. *Principal, 72*(3), 13–15.

Conner, D. R. (1992). *Managing at the speed of change: How resilient managers succeed and prosper where others fail.* New York: Villard Books.

Cuban, L. (1993). Computers meet classroom: Classroom wins. *Teachers College Record, 95*(2), 185–210.

Dalheim, M. (1994). *Time Strategies.* West Haven, CT: National Education Association of the United States.

Deal, T. E., & Kennedy, A. A. (1982). *Corporate cultures: The rites and rituals of corporate life.* Reading, MA: Addison-Wesley.

Donaldson, G. A. Jr. (1991). *Learning to teach.* New York: Greenwood Press.

Donahoe, T. (1993, December). Finding the way: Structure, time and culture in school improvement. *Phi Delta Kappan, 75*(4), 298–305.

DeFour, R. P. (1991). *The principal as staff developer.* Bloomington, IN: National Education Service.

DuFour, R., & Baker, R. (1992). *Creating the new American school: A principal's guide to school improvement.* Bloomington, IN: National Educational Service.

EduSolve (1996). *Advanced solutions for school management* (Brochure). Dallas, TX.

Elmore, R. F. (1995). Structural reform and educational practice. *Educational Researcher, 24*(9), 23–26.

Fullan, M. G. (1990). Staff development, innovation and institutional development. In B. Joyce (ed.). *Changing school culture through staff development* (pp. 3–25). Alexandria, VA: Association for Supervision and Curriculum Development.

Fullan, M. G. (1993). *Change forces: Probing the depths of educational reform.* New York: The Falmer Press.

Fullan, M. (1996, December). *School change: What's worth fighting for out there.* Distinguished Lecture Series, 28th Annual Conference of the National Staff Development Center, Vancouver, British Columbia.

Fullan, M. G., & Miles, M. B. (1992). Getting reform right: What works and what doesn't. *Phi Delta Kappan, 73*(10), 745–752.

Fullan, M. G., & Stiegelbauer, S. (1991). *The new meaning of educational change* (2nd ed.). New York: Teachers College Press.

George, P., & Lawrence, G. (1982). *A handbook for middle school teaching.* Glenview, IL: Scott, Foresman and Company.

Glickman, C. D., Gordon, S. P., & Ross-Gordon, J. M. (1995). *Supervision of instruction* (3rd ed.). Boston: Allyn & Bacon.

Goodlad, J. (1984). *A place called school: Prospects for the future.* New York: McGraw-Hill Publishing Company.

Guier, K. (1996). Reading teachers as change facilitators: A cross-site case study. Unpublished doctoral dissertation, Texas A&M-Commerce.

Guskey, T. R., & Kifer, E. (1995, April). *Evaluation of a high school block schedule restructuring program.* Paper presented at the annual meeting of the American Educational Research Association, San Francisco, CA.

Hackman, D. (1995, November). Ten guidelines for implementing block scheduling. *Educational Leadership, 53*(3), 24–27.

Handy, C. (1989). *The age of unreason.* Boston, MA: Harvard Business School Press.

Hanson, B. (1996). *McGraw-Hill School Systems' master schedule building workshop manual.* Monterey, CA.

Hart, L. E., Pate, P. E., Mizelle, N. P., & Reeves, J. E. (1982). Interdisciplinary team development in the middle school: A study of the Delta Project. *Research in Middle Level Education, 16*(1), 80–96.

Harvey, T. R. (1990). *Checklist for change: A pragmatic approach to creating and controlling change.* Boston: Allyn & Bacon.

Holleman, I. T., Jr. (1974). *The Trump Plan and the utilization of the differentiated staff* (NIE Publication No. EA 008 559, pp. 2–19). Washington, DC: U.S. Department of Health, Education and Welfare.

Hord, S. M. (1992) *Facilitative leadership: The imperative for change.* Austin, TX: Southwest Educational Development Laboratory.

Hord, S. M. (1995). *Change processes: Creating a content for change – Issue II.* Austin, TX: Texas Association for Supervision and Curriculum Development.

Hord, S. M., Rutherford, W. L., Huling-Austin, L., & Hall, G. E. (1987). *Taking charge of change.* Alexandria, VA: Association for Supervision and Curriculum Development.

Houston, P. D., Carter, G. R., Sava, S. G., & Dyer, T. J. (1995). *NCATE guidelines: Curriculum guidelines for advanced programs in educational leadership for principals, superintendents, curriculum directors, and supervisors.* Alexandria, VA: Association for Supervision and Curriculum Development.

Hughes, J. M. (1957). *Human Relations in Educational Organization.* New York: Harper and Brothers, Publishers.

Hughes, L. W., & Ubben, G. C. (1980). *The secondary principal's handbook.* Boston: Allyn & Bacon.

Hunter, M. (1987). *Mastery teaching.* El Segundo, CA: TIP Publications.

Hurt, J. (1992). Opening Pandora's box. *Educational Facility Planner, 30*(3), 14–18.

Jacobs, H. H. (1989). *Interdisciplinary curriculum: Design and implementation.* Alexandria, VA: Association for Supervision and Curriculum Development.

Jenkins, D. M., & Jenkins, K. D. (1991). The NMSA Delphi report: Roadmaps to the future. *Middle School Journal, 22*(4), 27–36.

Joyce, B., Showers, B., & Rolheiser-Bennett, C. (1987). Staff development and student learning: A synthesis of research on models of teaching. *Educational Leadership, 45*(2), 11–23.

Joyce, B., & Weil, M. (1986). Models of teaching (3rd ed.). Englewood Cliffs, NJ: Prentice Hall.

Joyce, B., Weil, M., & Showers, B. (1992). *Models of teaching* (4th ed.). Boston: Allyn & Bacon.

Kagan, J. (1971). A conception of early adolescence, *Daedalus 100,* 997–1012.

Kotter, J. P. (1996). *Leading change.* Boston, MA: Harvard Business School Press.

Keefe, J. W. (1971, January). Differentiated staffing – Its rewards and pitfalls. Paper presented at the National Association of Secondary School Principals Annual Convention, Houston, TX.

Kentta, B. (1993). The challenge of an integrated curriculum. *The School Administrator, 3*(50), 17–19.

Kruse, C. A., & Kruse, G. D. (1995, May). The master schedule and learning: Improving the quality of education. *NASSP Bulletin, 79*(571), 1–8.

Lipham, J. M., Rankin, R. E., & Hoeh, J. A., Jr. (1985). *The principalship.* New York: Longman Inc.

Lorain, P. (1996). More than a scenery change: What it takes to move from junior highs to middle schools. *The School Adminstrator, 53*(6), 13–17.

Lunenburg, F. C., & Ornstein, A. C. (1996). *Educational administration* (2nd ed.). Belmont, CA: Wadsworth Publishing Company.

MacIver, D. J. (1990). Meeting the needs of young adolescents: Advisory groups, interdisciplinary teaming teams, and school transition programs. *Phi Delta Kappan, 71,* 458–464.

Mager, R. F., & Pipe, P. (1984). *Analyzing performance problems or you really oughta wanna* (2nd ed.). Belmont, CA: Pitman Learning.

Macro Educational Systems, Inc. (1996). *SASIxp mass scheduling training guide* (Brochure). Laguna Hills, CA.

McGraw-Hill School Systems (1996). *The school system* (Brochure). Monterey, CA.

McPartland, J. M. (1989). *Balancing high quality subject-matter instruction with positive teacher–student relations in the middle grades* (Report No. OERI-G-86-0006). Washington, DC: Office of Educational Research and Improvement (ERIC Document Reproduction Service No. ED 291 704).

Mendez-Morse, S. (1992). *Leadership characteristics that facilitate school change.* Austin, TX: Southwest Educational Development Laboratory.

Merenbloom, E. Y. (1991). *The team process.* Columbus, OH: National Middle School Association.

Miles, M. B. & Louis, K. S. (1990). Mustering the will and skill for change. *Educational Leadership, 47*(8), 57–61.

National Association of Secondary School Principals' Commission on Restructuring (1992). *A leader's guide to school restructuring,* Reston, VA: NASSP.

National Commission on Teaching and America's Future (1996). *What matters most: Teaching for America's future.* Washington, DC: Government Printing Service.

National Computing Systems, Inc. (1995). *NCS comprehensive information management for schools III* (Brochure). Minneapolis, MN.

National Education Commission on Time and Learning (1994). *Prisoners of time.* Washington, DC: Government Printing Office.

Nottingham, M. A. (1977). *Principles for principals.* Washington, DC: University Press of America.

Pankake, A. M. (1996). Change and technology leadership. Two sides of the same coin. *Educational Considerations, 23*(2), 25–28.

Pankake, A. M., & Palmer, B. (1996). Making the connections: Linking staff development interventions to implementation of full inclusion. *Journal of Staff Development, 17*(3), 26–30.

Peters, R. O. (1993). Student self-scheduling to meet the goals of 21st century education. *Schools in the Middle, 2*(3), 40–44.

Pogrow, S. (1996). Reforming the wannabe reformers: Why education reforms almost always end up making things worse. *Phi Delta Kappan, 77*(10), 656–663.

Pritchett, P. (1996). *Mindshift.* Dallas, TX: Pritchett & Associates.

Raywid, M. A. (1993). Finding time for collaboration. *Educational Leadership, 51*(1), 30–34.

Reid, W. M., Hierck, T., & Veregin, L. (1994). Measurable gains of block scheduling. *The School Administrator, 51*(3), 32–33.

Richardson, J. (1996, November). Teacher knowledge, skills most important influences on student learning. *The Developer.* Oxford, OH: National Staff Development Council.

Rifkin, J., & Howard, T. (1980). *Entropy: A new world*. New York: The Viking Press.

Rosenshine, B. V. (1986). Synthesis of research on explicit teaching. *Educational Leadership, 43*(7), 60–69.

Rossow, L. F. (1990). *The principalship: Dimensions in instructional leadership*. Englewood Cliffs, NJ: Prentice Hall.

Sadowski, M. (1986). Just like starting over: The promises and pitfalls of block scheduling. *The Harvard Education Letter, 12*(6), 1–3.

Sarason, S. B. (1990). *The predictable failure of educational reform*. San Francisco, CA: Jossey-Bass Pub.

Sarason, S. B. (1996). *Revisiting "the culture of the school and the problem of change."* New York: Teachers College Press.

Schlechty, P. C. (1990). *Schools for the 21st century: Leadership imperatives for educational reform*. San Francisco, CA: Jossey-Bass.

Schlechty, P. C., & Cole, R. W. (1992). Creating "Standard-Bearer Schools." *Educational Leadership, 50*(3), 45–49.

Schroth, G., & Dunbar, R. (1993, Fall). Mission Possible: One school's journey to site-based decision making. *Catalyst for Change (23),* 24–26.

Schroth, G., & Dixon, J. (1996, July). The effects of block scheduling on student performance. *International Journal of Educational Reform, 5*(4), 472–476.

Scott, C. D., & Jaffe, D. T. (1989). *Managing organizational change: A practical guide for managers*. Menlo, CA: Crisp Publications.

Senge, P. M. (1990). *The fifth discipline: The art and practice of the learning organization*. New York: Doubleday–A Currency Book.

Sergiovanni, T. J. (1995). *The principalship: A reflective practice perspective* (3rd ed.). Boston: Allyn & Bacon.

Sergiovanni, T. J., & Starratt, R. J. (1993). *Supervision: A redefinition*. New York: McGraw-Hill, Inc.

Shortt, T. L., & Thayer, Y. (1995, May). What can we expect to see in the next generation of block scheduling? *NASSP Bulletin, 79*(571), 53–65.

Sizer, T. R. (1986). Rebuilding: First steps by the Coalition of Essential Schools. *Phi Delta Kappan, 68*(1), 38–42.

Sizer, T. R. (1992). *Horaces' school: Redesigning the American high school*. Boston: Houghton Mifflin Company.

Slavin, R. E. (1993, May). Ability grouping in the middle grades: Achievement effects and alternatives. *The Elementary School Journal, 93*(5), 535–552.

Slavin, R. E., & Karweit, N. A. (1989). *Effective programs for students at risk*. Boston: Allyn & Bacon.

Software Technology, Inc. (1996). *The student scheduling and tracking system* (Brochure). Mobile, AL.

Sommerfeld, M. (1993, March 13). Time and space. *Education Week,* 13–19.

Sparks, D., & Loucks-Horsley, S. (1990). *Five models of staff development for teachers*. Oxford, OH: National Staff Development Council.

Spear, R. C. (1992). Middle level team scheduling: Appropriate grouping for adolescents. *Schools in the Middle, 2*(1), 30–34.

Spencer, W. A., & Lowe, C. (1994, November). *The use of block periods for instruction: A report and evaluation*. Paper presented at the Annual Meeting of the Mid-South Educational Research Association, Nashville, TN.

Surfside Software, Inc. (1995). *The surfside solution III schedule module for IBM compatible computers* (Brochure). East Orleans, MA.
Swaim, S. (1996, June). The central office role in middle-level school reform. *The School Administrator, 6*(53), 6–9.
Texas Educational Consultative Services, Inc. (1996). *Scheduling software* (Brochure). Austin, TX.
Tozloski, J. H. (1995, September). Making math fun! *Schools in the Middle, 5*(1), 12.
Trump, J. L. (April, 1958). An image of the future in improved staff utilization. *Bulletin of the National Association of Secondary School Principals, XLII,* 324–329.
Trump, J. L. (1977). *School for everyone.* Reston, VA: National Association for Secondary School Principals.
Tyack, D., & Cuban, L. (1996). *Tinkering toward utopia: A century of public school reform.* Cambridge, MA: Harvard University Press.
Ubben, G. C. (1976). A third block schedule. *NASSP Bulletin, 60*(397), 104–111.
Ubben, G. C., & Hughes, L. W. (1992). *The principal* (2nd ed.). Boston: Allyn & Bacon.
Van Dyke, R., & Stallings, M. A. (1995). How to build an inclusive school community. *Phi Delta Kappan, 76*(6), 475–479.
Vroom, V. H., & Jago, A. G. (1988). *The new leadership: Managing participation in organizations.* Englewood Cliffs, NJ: Prentice-Hall.
Watts, G. D., & Castle, S. (1993). The time dilemma in school restructuring. *Phi Delta Kappan, 75*(4), 306–310.
Wheatley, M. J. (1992). *Leadership and the new science: Learning about organization from an orderly universe.* San Francisco, CA: Berrett-Koehler Publishers, Inc.
Wilson, C. (1995). The 4:4 block system: A workable alternative. *NASSP Bulletin, 79*(571), 63–65.
Wood, C. L., Nicholson, E. W., & Findley, D. G. (1979). *The secondary school principal: Manager and supervisor.* Boston: Allyn & Bacon, Inc.
Wood, C. L., Nicholson, E. W., & Findley, D. G. (1985). *The secondary school principal: Manager and supervisor* (2nd ed.). Boston: Allyn & Bacon.

FILMS, GAMES, AND OTHER MATERIALS

Making Change for School Improvement (i.e., the "change game") is available from The NETWORK (300 Brickstone Square, Suite 900, Andover, MA 01810; 800-877-5400). This is a simulation game that allows players to involve themselves in trying to implement a program in a fictional school district. It is a worry-free way to practice some change strategies and explore the consequences of the behaviors. A new simulation, Systems Thinking/Systems Changing, is now also available from The NETWORK.

CRM Films has some videos on an array of topics (teamwork, quality, leadership, conflict management, communication, and diversity). All of these topics have some relationship to change and the change process. However, they also have films that address change directly, for example

- Leadership and the New Science
- Creating a Capacity for Change: Phillip Schlecty on the Future of Education

CRM Films is located at 2215 Faraday Avenue, Carlsbad, CA 92008-9829; phone: 800-421-0833.

Windows of Change video featuring Jennifer James is a combination of important content and entertaining presentation. It is available from Enterprise Media, Inc., 91 Harvey Street, Cambridge, MA 02140; phone: 617-354-0017.

Pritchett and Associates, Inc. have numerous publications on change. These publications are brief but very informational. Pritchett and Associates, Inc., is located at 13155 Noel Road, Suite 1600, Dallas, TX 75240.

Southwest Educational Development Laboratory located in Austin, Texas, continues to produce some of the best research and training materials on change and the change process. Many of the research reports and some training sessions are available directly from SEDL. To contact representatives: Southwest Educational Development Laboratory, 211 E. 7th Street, Austin, TX 78701; phone: 512-467-6861.

INDEX

Assessment, 7, 9, 14
  of needs, 41
Assignment
  students to classes, 40, 42
Athletics, 45, 50, 84, 85, 87, 89

Band, 87
BEGGS, xv
BELL, 4
Bells, 90
  schedule, 96
BLACK, 4, 99
Block scheduling, xvii, 11, 14, 49, 52
  75-30-75, 88
  75-30-75 Plan, 58
  advantages, 51, 55, 94, 96
  alternate day, 54, 83
  disadvantages, 51, 56, 99
  double block, 83
  elementary schools, 93-97
  flexible, 54, 85, 96, 99
  fluid, xvi, 55, 87-88
  guidelines, 102
  modified, 102
  parallel, 58, 88, 93, 97
    advantages, 98
  semester, 57, 87
  trimester, 59, 88
BOYD, 30
BROPHY, 9
Budget, 40, 57, 62, 103
BURNS, 22

CANADY, 42, 58, 97, 98
Carnegie Report, xvi-xvii, 3, 42, 59
Carnegie Unit, xiv, xvi
Central office
  approval, 68
  support, 48, 57, 62, 103
Chancery Software Ltd., 116
Change, 19-38, 47, 97, 99, 103
  advocacy for, 31
  ambiguity of, 28
  analyzing, 25
  barriers to, 104
  benefits of, 22
  clarity, 22
  commitment to, 24-25
  desired, 22
  elementary schools, 95
  expectations, 26
  implementation, 24
  in elementary schools, 92
  momentum, 29
  monitoring, 31
  motivation to, 22
  needed, 22
  normative, 10
  phases, 27
  preparation for, 21, 23, 33
  readiness for, 21
  reinforcing, 26
  speed of, 21
  structural, 10
  unexpected results, 32
  useful, 28

127

Class periods
  50 minute, xiv, 52, 89, 95
  60 minutes, 50
  90 minute, xvii, 14, 49, 83
Class rosters, 80
Class sections
  multiple, 74
Class size, 58, 59, 97
Classroom
  availability, 68
  rules, 8
  self-contained
    advantages, 51
Community
  support, 48, 57, 62
Computer programs, 68, 84, 111
  (SASI) III, 112
  EduSolve, 111
  Mac School Student Information System, 111
  Macro Educational Systems, Inc., 112
  Management for Schools III, 114
  McGraw-Hill School Systems, 113
  Modular Management System for Schools, 114
  SASIxp, 112
  Student Scheduling and Tracking System, 115
  Surfside Solution III, 115
  Texas Educational Consultative Services, Inc. 116
  The Elementary School System, 113
  Win School Information System, 116
Conflict matrix, 71, 75
CONNER, 20, 22
Cooperative learning, 2, 7, 14, 96
Costs, 24, 25
Course, 49
  booklets, 69
  conflicts, 75
  constraints, 74
  listings, 45
  offerings, 40, 45, 69
  requests, 68, 78, 80
    editing, 71
  required, 68
  sections, 71

tallies, 70
Curriculum, 2, 6, 95
  advertising, 68

Daily demand schedule, xvi
DALHEIM, xii
Disabled students, 89
Distance learning, 46
DIXON, 14, 49, 50
Doubleton, 74
Doubletons, 75
DOYLE, 29
DuFOUR, 22, 31
DUNBAR, 2

Electives, 45, 50, 68, 69, 70, 88, 89, 90
Elementary
  school scheduling, 92
  schools, xiv, 95
  students, 3, 4
    attention span, 95
ELMORE, 11
Enrollment, 68
Evaluation, 104

FINDLEY, xv, xvi
FOGLIANI, 97
FULLAN, 10, 11, 20, 23, 24, 25, 27, 28, 29, 30, 32, 33
Funding, 104

GEORGE, 5
Gifted, 89, 93, 97, 100
GLICKMAN, 7, 11, 12
GOODLAD, 96
GORDON, 7, 11, 12
Grouping, 61
  by ability, 41, 50
  heterogeneous, 48, 50, 89, 98
  homogeneous, 98

GUSKEY, 14, 49

HACKMAN, 62, 102, 103, 104
HALL, 25, 30
Hand scheduling, 66
HANSON, 68

HARVEY, 22, 23, 27, 31
HIERCK, 11
HOLLEMAN, xiv
Homework, 8–9
HORD, 25, 30
HOUSTON, xii
HUGHES, xv, xvi, 7, 8, 42
HULING-AUSTIN, 25, 30
HUNTER, 8

Instruction, 1, 6
  individualized, xv, 52, 61, 101
  instructional goals, 1
  objectives, 9
Interdisciplinary, xv, 2, 5, 7, 60, 88, 96, 101
Itinerant teachers, 44, 52, 85, 87

JACOBS, 60
JAMES, 5
JOYCE, 7

KEEFE, xv
KENTTA, 1
KIFER, 14, 49
KOTTER, 22, 27

LAWRENCE, 5, 12
LOUCKS-HORSLEY, 12, 23
LOUIS, 23, 24, 25
LOWE, 49
Lunch, 83, 87, 94, 101
Lunch periods, 46, 72
LUNENBURG, 47

MAC IVER, 60
Master schedule, 42
  construction, 65–90
    rules, 75
  materials, 72
MCPARTLAND, 41
MERENBLOOM, 2, 14, 49, 60, 89
Middle school
  students, 3
MILES, 11, 23, 24, 25, 32
Modular scheduling, xv–xvi, 56

NASSP, 94
National Commission on Teaching and America's Future, 30, 97
National Computer Systems, Inc., 114
National Education Commission on Time and Learning, 95
NCATE, xii
NICHOLSON, xv, xvi

Open schools, xv
ORNSTEIN, 47

PALMER, 29
PANKAKE, 21, 25, 27, 29
Parent
  attitudes, 40
  involvement, 70
  meetings, 70
  pressure, 49
  support, 57, 62
Planning, 7, 57
  periods, 43, 44, 49, 55, 62, 68, 94, 99
  schedule, 68
POGROW, xiii, 2, 29
PONDER, 29
PRITCHETT, 22, 24
Program
  needs, 68
PUCKETT, 4

Quadrupletons, 75

Recess, 94
Reform, 48, 93, 94
Register students, 68, 70
REID, 11
Release periods, 68
Reports, 80
Research, 48
Resistance, 27
Resources, 24, 32, 104
RETTIG, 42, 58
Revolving period schedule, xvi
RICHARDSON, 30
RIFKIN, 30, 32

ROGERS, 4, 99
ROLHEISER-BENNETT, 7
Room assignments, 80
ROSS-GORDON, 7, 11, 12
RUTHERFORD, 25, 30

SARASON, 2
Schedule
　challenges, 40
　choices, 14, 68
　distribution, 80
　　historical perspective, xiv
　lock in, 80
　printed, 80
　problems, 40
School
　climate, 42
　size, 50
SCHROTH, 2, 14, 49, 50
Seat count, 76
SERGIOVANNI, 8, 10, 13, 47
Shared decision making, 45, 47
SHORTT, 14
SHOWERS, 7
Singletons, 74, 75
SIZER, 11, 95
SLAVIN, 50
SOMMERFELD, xii
Space, xiv
Special education, 43, 49, 93, 94, 97, 100
Special programs, 100
　flexibly scheduling, 99
　　advantages, 101
Specialists, 44, 52, 94, 97
SPENCER, 49
Split classes, 46
Staff development, 3, 7, 10-15, 23, 57, 62, 103, 104
　in service, 13
　renewal, 13
　stages, 13
Stakeholders, 103
STARRATT, 8, 10, 13
Student
　population, 41
Student achievement, 8, 9, 11, 41, 49

Student behavior, 42, 52, 101
Student needs, 2, 3
　elementary, 3, 93
　　intellectual, 4
　　physical, 4
　　social/emotional, 4
　middle school, 5
　　intellectual, 6
　　physical, 5
　　social/emotional, 5
Systems, 103

Teacher
　attitudes, 40, 45
　certification, 68
　commitment, 47
　conflict, 89
　involvement, 13, 47
　qualifications, 68
　requests, 68
　student ratio, 71, 96, 97
　training, 14, 15
Teaching, 2, 9
　activities, 52
　assignments, 42, 44
　behaviors, 8-9
　effective, 7, 11
　methods, 2, 57
Teaming, xv, xvii, 15, 43, 49, 50, 59, 60, 89, 97, 101
　advantages, 51, 60
　disadvantages, 51, 62
　flexibly blocked, 60
　planning, 88
　scheduling, 88
　school within a school, 90
　student placement, 50
　teaching, 7, 96, 101
Technology, 66
THAYER, 14
Time, xii, xiv, 2, 8, 11, 26, 30, 68, 96
　engaged, 9
　line, 68
Title I, 93, 94, 97, 100, 101
　tracking, 41
Traditional scheduling, 87-88
　advantages, 51

disadvantages, 51–52
elementary schools, 93
Transver students, 57
Tripletons, 75–78
TRUMP, xiv
  plan, xv
Trust, 44, 47
Tutorials, 87

UBBEN, xv, xvi, 7, 8, 42

VEREGIN, 11

WEIL, 7
WOOD, xv, xvi, 47

Zero Period schedule, xvi